Bram Stoker ◆ Roberta Simpson Brown
Adèle Geras ◆ Maria Leach ◆ Stephen King
Evelyn Waugh ◆ Edgar Allan Poe ◆ Felix Boyd
Frederic Brown ◆ Agatha Christie

Amazing
Characters

by Guglielmo Corrado

Editors: Monika Marszewska, Rebecca Raynes, Elvira Poggi Repetto
Design: Nadia Maestri

Cover illustration and illustrations on pages 74, 111 and 115 by Gianni De Conno

The author wishes to thank the editors for their competence, suggestions, patience and careful work. He also thanks his colleagues and all those who have helped and encouraged him.

We have made every effort to publish this book free of errors. Please let us know if you notice any we have overlooked. We would also be grateful for suggestions and observations.
editorial@blackcat-cideb.com
www.blackcat-cideb.com
www.cideb.it

CISQ CERT
TEXTBOOKS AND
TEACHING MATERIALS
The quality of the publisher's
design, production and sales processes has
been certified to the standard of
UNI EN ISO 9001

Black Cat Publishing is an imprint of Cideb Editrice.

ISBN 978-88-7754-375-2

Printed in Italy by Litoprint, Genoa

CONTENTS

PHONETIC SYMBOLS

Vowels

[ɪ]	*as in*	six
[i]	"	happy
[iː]	"	see
[e]	"	red
[æ]	"	hat
[ɑː]	"	car
[ɒ]	"	dog
[ɔː]	"	door
[ʊ]	"	put
[uː]	"	food
[ʌ]	"	cup
[ə]	"	about
[ɜː]	"	girl

Diphthongs

[eɪ]	*as in*	made
[aɪ]	"	five
[aʊ]	"	house
[ɔɪ]	"	boy
[əʊ]	"	home
[ɪə]	"	beer
[eə]	"	hair
[ʊə]	"	poor

Consonants

[b]	*as in*	bed
[k]	"	cat
[tʃ]	"	church
[d]	"	day
[f]	"	foot
[g]	"	good
[dʒ]	"	page
[h]	"	how
[j]	"	yes
[l]	"	leg
[m]	"	mum
[n]	"	nine
[ŋ]	"	sing
[p]	"	pen
[r]	"	red
[s]	"	soon
[z]	"	zoo
[ʃ]	"	show
[ʒ]	"	measure
[t]	"	tea
[θ]	"	thin
[ð]	"	this
[v]	"	voice
[w]	"	wine

[']   represents primary stress in the syllable which follows

[ˌ]   represents secondary stress in the syllable which follows

[r]   indicates that the final "r" is only pronounced before a word beginning with a vowel sound (British English). In American English, the "r" is usually pronounced before both consonants and vowel sounds.

ORGANISATION

The *Amazing Characters* pack includes:

• a textbook

• an audiocassette

The pack is addressed to **intermediate learners** and provides a wide source of literary and linguistic materials. The textbook includes <u>nine short stories</u> and a <u>selection of extracts</u> from Bram Stoker's *Dracula*.

The stories are introduced by a brief panoramic view on the origins, development and varieties of the short story.

The choice of the texts is based on the following reasons: they focus on communication, offer a high point of language usage, favour interaction and are open to multiple interpretation.

The **short story** is analysed as a highly motivating genre distinct from the novel, which has unity of effect and is perhaps the best way to guide the students to understand the combination of contents and stylistic features. The students will be helped to understand the basic structure of the short story and will be gradually led to appreciate its numerous variations while focusing on their favourite characters. Furthermore, they will read some **unabridged extracts** taken from Bram Stoker's *Dracula* and will be able to get a general idea of the whole work, thanks to the summary-links between some extracts.

Each story is preceded by information on the author, followed by a list of his/her main works. **Cross-Curricular Data** help the students to contextualize what they are reading, while focusing their attention on the story-variety they are analysing.

The itinerary proposed is **thematic** and the stories have been divided into three Units which are self-contained: **horrifying**, **irrational** and **unforgettable characters.** However, the structure of the book is **modular**, so each unit may be read in casual order and each story may be analysed separately; therefore, the teacher may feel free to create his/her own itineraries within the text.

At the basis of this approach there is the interaction with literary texts involving the students in stimulating activities. These develop their spirit of discovery, expand vocabulary and general linguistic competence and show that learning can be something stimulating and challenging even when working with literary texts.

The stories and extracts included in this book have been split into sections to make them as accessible as possible; the **activities** are graded and progress from familiarisation with the text to analysis, synthesis and free production. All the activities are student-oriented and aim at developing the main study skills: listening, reading for general information, looking for specific information, taking notes, summarising, gap-filling, analysing characters and behaviour, discussing in pairs or in groups, creating word-files, etc. While interacting with the text, the students are required to perform particular tasks, which help them understand how words work on the page to establish meaning and to convey messages.

The **Overview** at the end of the book guides the students to fill in a **Reference-Table** about what they have read, enables them to compare/contrast/group the characters and asks them to express their opinions on the whole book.

The accompanying **audiocassette**, which includes extracts from *Dracula* and five of the stories recorded by native speakers, helps to improve comprehension skills and promotes appreciation of the texts while providing a model for accuracy in pronunciation and further exposure to real language.

Guglielmo Corrado

THE SHORT STORY

Origins

Short fiction has existed since the beginnings of literature and its origins can be traced back to Homer's *Odyssey* in old times, Boccaccio's *Decameron* and Chaucer's *Canterbury Tales* in the Middle Ages and Defoe's *A True Revelation of the Apparition of One Mrs Veal* in the 18th century. However, until the 19th century, short fiction was normally part of longer narratives.

As an independent literary genre, the short story actually started in American magazines published at the beginning of the 19th century: the tales included were different in length and style and were mainly anonymous.

In his essay *Twice-Told Tales by Nathaniel Hawthorn. A Review* (1842), Edgar Allan Poe gave importance to the short story on the literary scene:

'...if any literary work is too long to be read at one sitting, we must be content to dispense with the immensely important effect derivable from unity of impression – for, if two sittings be required, the affairs of the world interfere and everything like totality is at once destroyed.'

Poe maintained that the short story should have a 'certain unique or single effect' that writers had to keep in mind throughout narration, if they really wanted to impress it on the reader's mind.

Development

The 19th Century

The short story gradually changed, becoming more realistic: the works of the Russian writer Anton Chekhov and of the French writer Guy de Maupassant are famous examples.

In his essay *The Philosophy of the Short Story* (1884), the American critic Brander Matthews analysed the main characteristics of the short story and claimed that its 'symmetry of design' was an important distinguishing feature and that writers could achieve it by focusing on a character, an event or an emotion.

Some years later, O. Henry concentrated on the conclusion of the short story so much so that since then, the term 'O. Henryism' has been used to refer to any tale with a surprise ending. In his stories O. Henry's 'formula' was a carefully planned plot with a sudden conclusion that reversed the initial situation.

The 20th Century

At the beginning of the 20th century the 'formula' story disappeared because writers became aware that a short story could do without even a beginning or a conclusion.

The change was also a reflection of the technological, scientific, economic and political innovations in the world. Thus, the classical structure of the short story became fragmented, its focus was directed on real life and its conclusion was opened to multiple interpretations. There was no longer a presentation of events in chronological order or a logical sequence of cause and effect, but rather the unfolding of a series of impressions. Writers like Virginia Woolf concentrated on the characters' mental state, their behaviour and their moments of crisis: the outside world lost importance in comparison with the inner world of characters.

Impressionist painting, Freud's theories on the unconscious and the importance he gave to dreams and sex, together with photography and films considerably influenced fiction in this period.

When Impressionism evolved into Expressionism and Symbolism in visual art, writers realised that it was impossible to give a realistic and objective portrayal of reality. As a consequence they started to give symbolic representations of the world.

An outstanding example is *Dubliners* (1914) by James Joyce, where the author presented 'snapshots' of life in the form of 'epiphanies' or 'sudden spiritual manifestations': the writer's focus shifted from the traditional sequence of episodes to the effects that actions have on the individual mind.

The 1960's were marked by the development of the 'Absurd', which was characterised by a meaningless plot, destruction of the traditional time-sequence and a presentation of impressions. Perhaps the most famous writer of this genre was Samuel Beckett.

It is difficult to define exactly what the short story became afterwards. It is no doubt relevant what M. Bradbury said in his Introduction to the *Penguin Book of Modern British Short Stories*:

> '…the writer is saying something crucial about the form he or she is using, as well as treating a subject or distilling an experience. Recent writers have emphasised this greatly and given the short story a remarkable contemporary promise.'

Main sub-genres

anecdote	a short, amusing account of something that has happened
fairy tale	a story centred on magic, fairies, elves, etc. usually for children
parable	a brief story using symbols to illustrate a moral or religious point
shaggy dog	a long story, usually amusing, which has a deliberately weak or meaningless ending
sketch	a brief description of a character with an interesting personality
tall tale	an unlikely narration of events that the narrator does not expect will be believed
vignette	a short effective description of a character or a scene

Note down:

1 the origins of the short story.

2 the reason why short stories should be read 'at one sitting' according to E.A. Poe.

3 the meaning of 'symmetry of design'.

4 the use of the term 'O. Henryism'.

5 the reason/s for the disappearance of the 'formula' story at the beginning of the 20th century.

6 how the structure of the short story changed in the 20th century.

7 the meaning of the term 'epiphany'.

8 the features of the 'Absurd'.

Varieties

The Gothic Story

Gothic tales dealt with murders, supernatural events and extraordinary situations and were mainly set in haunted castles, prisons and Gothic buildings. Gothic writers discovered the charm of horror and were influenced by the theories of the philosopher E. Burke on the sublime and the beautiful.

The Horror Story

The origins of this genre can be found in the Gothic novel. Themes such as vampirism, the eruption of ancient evil, monstrous transformations, etc. were first used by horror writers. Elements of terror in the form of supernatural entities (aliens, odd creatures, possessed people or machinery) have become part of modern horror stories.

The Ghost Story

Folklore, myths and ancient legends are the main sources of inspiration for this type of story, which is based on mysterious events and apparitions that do not have any logical explanation. It is centred on the influence that the spirits of the dead have in the world of the living.

The Science Fiction Story

Nuclear power, space exploration, computer science and medical discoveries are at the basis of this type of story whose main purpose is to change standard perceptions of reality by dealing with alternatives: future events, robots, aliens, utopias and dystopias, space and time travel, etc.

The Detective Story

It is based on a detective's investigations into a crime. The detective stands out from the other characters for his/her capabilities and is generally helped by a less able assistant.

Note down:

the main features of the story-types analysed.

GLOSSARY

Author: the person who writes the book.

Characters: can be **flat** or **round**. (see page 178)

Climax: the moment of highest intensity in a text.

Epiphany: a sudden spiritual revelation.

In medias res: a narration which starts in the middle of a scene or a situation, without an introduction.

Linkers: conjunctions, adverbs and expressions which connect sentences in a logical way.

Keyword: a word which is either essential or very important in conveying meaning in a text.

Metaphor: figure of speech in which one thing is indirectly compared to another (without the use of words such as *like* or *as*).

Point of view: the position a narrator takes when telling a story (internal or external to the narration, etc.).

Plot: the way in which the sequence of events of a story are told.

Setting: the background (place, time, etc.) of an action.

Scanning: reading a text carefully to find specific information.

Simile: figure of speech by which one thing is directly compared to another, often introduced by *like* or *as*.

Skimming: reading a text quickly to get the gist or overall meaning.

Story: chronological sequence of events that make up a literary text.

Style: the way in which language is used by a writer to express his/her ideas, or views.

A Cinema Poem

I like it when
They get shot in the head
And there's blood on the pillow
And blood on the bed

And it's good when
They get stabbed in the eye
And they scream and they take
A long time to die

And it all spurts out
All over the floor
And the audience shivers
And shouts for more
But I don't like it when they kiss.

(From Roger McGough's *Sky in the Pie*)

UNIT ONE

Horrifying Characters

"You are entering a Supernatural world..."

Dracula

by Bram Stoker

Bram Stoker

Abraham Stoker was born in Dublin, in 1847. He was greatly influenced by his mother, who was an active social worker, feminist, writer and great storyteller. Since Stoker was often bedridden as a child, she told him gruesome Irish horror stories. It is said that Stoker's taste for the unusual and the supernatural began in this period.

He was educated at the University of Dublin, where he distinguished himself as an athlete and football player.

As a young man, he followed in his mother's footsteps and wrote in defence of women's rights. Later, however, he changed his attitude. He was interested in the poems by Walt Whitman, with whom he established an intense correspondence.

He joined the Irish Civil Service in 1866 and in 1870 he began his career as a civil servant in Dublin.

In 1876 he left Ireland and met his idol, the English actor Sir Henry Irving, becoming his secretary and manager two years later and joining him in the management of the Lyceum Theatre in London. He kept this post for twenty-seven years. He met and made friends with outstanding literary figures: Mark Twain, Walt Whitman, Alfred Tennyson and Oscar Wilde.

Stoker died in 1912.

Main works:

Dracula (1897)

The Jewel of the Seven Stars (1903)

Personal Reminiscences of Henry Irving (1906)

The Lady of the Shroud (1909)

The Lair of the White Worm (1911)

BACKGROUND INFORMATION

The title of the book derives from Vlad IV, Prince of Wallachia (1431-1476), who was the son of Vlad Dracul (or Vlad the Devil); 'Dracula' means 'Son of the Devil'. The origin of Dracula is thought to have been Vlad Tepes, or Vlad the Impaler, ruler of medieval Wallachia, who used to impale his victims and then mock them.

The book appeared in a period in which people were becoming more and more interested in stories dealing with ghosts, the supernatural and strange events.

However, Dracula was not the very first story about vampires: there had been, for instance, *Der Vampyr* by Heinrich Marschner, *The Castle of Otranto* by Horace Walpole and *The Mysteries of Udolpho* by Ann Radcliffe.

Stoker's original working notes of *Dracula* are exhibited in the Rosenbach Museum in Philadelphia.

SOMETHING ABOUT THE SETTING

One of the main settings of the story is Transylvania, a real country, situated between the west of Romania and the south of Hungary and which is surrounded by the Carpathians and the Transylvanian Alps on the east and south, and by the Bihor Mountains in the west.

Formerly a province, with its capital at Cluj, it was part of Hungary from about 1000 until its people voted to unite with Romania in 1918.

Poster from Francis Ford Coppola's film 'Dracula'.

Bram Stoker

BEFORE READING

1 Tick ✓ one or more of the following definitions and then discuss your choices with your classmates.

a A vampire is:

☐ the ghost of a dead wrongdoer

☐ a huge bat feeding on the blood of sleeping people

☐ a cannibal

☐ just an imaginary creature

☐ an un-dead creature

b People bitten by a vampire:

☐ die immediately

☐ die in a short time

☐ become vampires themselves

☐ change into beasts

☐ go on living as usual

c The only way to kill a vampire and set his/her soul free is:

☐ to shoot it with a silver bullet

☐ to drive a cross through the vampire's heart

☐ to use protective plants (e.g. garlic)

2 Read the following definitions taken from the *Webster's Concise Interactive Encyclopedia* to expand your knowledge on vampires:

Vampire

'Hungarian vampir (and similar forms in other Slavonic languages) in Hungarian and Slavonic folklore, an "undead" corpse that sleeps by day in its native earth, and by night, often in the form of a bat, sucks the blood of the living.'

Vampire Bat

'Any South and Central American bat of the family Desmodontidae, of which there are three species. The common vampire Desmodus rotundus is found from New Mexico to central Argentina; its head and body grow to 9 cm/3.5 in. Vampires feed on the blood of birds and mammals; they slice a piece of skin from a sleeping animal with their sharp incisor teeth and lap up the flowing blood.

Vampires feed on all kinds of mammals including horses, cattle, and occasionally humans. They fly low and settle on the ground before running to a victim. The bite is painless and the loss of blood is small; the victim seldom comes to any harm. Vampire bats are intelligent and among the few mammals to manifest altruistic behaviour (they adopt orphans and help other bats in need).'

Scene from Bram Stoker's 'Dracula' directed by Francis Ford Coppola, starring Keanu Reeves.

• •

The characters you will meet in these Extracts are:

DRACULA   Transylvanian Count

THREE YOUNG WOMEN   Vampires in the Castle

JONATHAN HARKER   a young solicitor

MINA   Jonathan's fiancée

MR MORRIS   an American friend

• •

Bram Stoker

Jonathan Harker goes to Count Dracula's castle in Transylvania to settle some business about the Count's purchase of the estate of Carfax in Essex.

EXTRACT ONE

From Jonathan Harker's Journal, Chapter 2.

1 The following Extract is taken from the beginning of the story when Jonathan Harker arrives at Dracula's castle. Read the first part and complete the following table.

What was unusual about Dracula's appearance	1.. 2..
Effect produced by the silver lamp	

• •

A key was turned with the loud grating [1] noise of long disuse, [2] and the great door swung back. [3]

Within, stood a tall old man, clean-shaven save [4] for a long white moustache, and clad [5] in black from head to foot, without a single speck of
5 colour about him anywhere. He held in his hand an antique silver lamp, in which the flame burned without chimney or globe [6] of any kind, throwing long, quivering shadows as it flickered [7] in the draught [8] of the open door.

• •

Continue reading, then answer the questions which follow.

1 **grating** : harsh, unpleasant.

2 **disuse** : state of not being used.

3 **swung back** : moved back.

4 **save** : except.

5 **clad** : clothed.

6 **chimney or globe** : glass tube which protects the flame of a lamp from draughts.

7 **flickered** : burnt unsteadily.

8 **draught** [drɑ:ft] : movement of air.

Dracula

The old man motioned me in with his right hand with a courtly gesture, saying in excellent English, but with a strange intonation: –

'Welcome to my house! Enter freely and of your own will!' He made no motion of stepping to meet me, but stood like a statue, as though his gesture of welcome had fixed him into stone. The instant, however, that I had stepped over the threshold,[1] he moved impulsively forward, and holding out his hand grasped[2] mine with a strength which made me wince,[3] an effect which was not lessened[4] by the fact that it seemed as cold as ice – more like the hand of a dead than a living man. Again he said: –

'Welcome to my house. Come freely. Go safely. And leave something of the happiness you bring!' The strength of the handshake was so much akin[5] to that which I had noticed in the driver, whose face I had not seen, that for a moment I doubted if it were not the same person to whom I was speaking; so, to make sure, I said interrogatively: –

'Count Dracula?' He bowed in a courtly way as he replied: –

'I am Dracula. And I bid you welcome, Mr Harker, to my house. Come in; the night air is chill,[6] and you must need to eat and rest.' As he was speaking he put the lamp on a bracket[7] on the wall, and stepping out, took my luggage; he had carried it in before I could forestall[8] him. I protested, but he insisted: –

'Nay, sir, you are my guest. It is late, and my people are not available. Let me see to your comfort myself.' He insisted on carrying my traps[9] along the passage, and then up a great winding[10] stair, and along another great passage, on whose stone floor our steps rang heavily. At the end of this he threw open a heavy door, and I rejoiced[11] to see within a well-lit room in which a table was spread for supper, and on whose mighty hearth[12] a great fire of logs flamed and flared.[13]

The Count halted, putting down my bags, closed the door, and crossing the room, opened another door, which led into a small octagonal room lit by a single lamp, and seemingly[14] without a window of any sort. Passing through

1	**threshold** [θreʃhəʊld] : doorway forming the entrance to the house.	8	**forestall** : stop.
2	**grasped** : held very firmly.	9	**traps** : baggage, luggage.
3	**wince** : jump with pain.	10	**winding** [wɪndɪŋ] : full of bends.
4	**lessened** : reduced.	11	**rejoiced** : felt happy.
5	**akin** [əkɪn] : similar.	12	**hearth** [hɑːθ] : floor of a fire place.
6	**chill** : cold.	13	**flared** : burnt with a bright light.
7	**bracket** : support.	14	**seemingly** : apparently.

this, he opened another door, and motioned me to enter. It was a welcome sight; for here was a great bedroom well lighted and warmed with another
40 log fire, which sent a hollow roar up the wide chimney. The Count himself left my luggage inside and withdrew, saying, before he closed the door:–

'You will need, after your journey, to refresh yourself by making your toilet. I trust you will find all you wish. When you are ready come into the other room, where you will find your supper prepared.'

45 The light and warmth and the Count's courteous welcome seemed to have dissipated all my doubts and fears. Having then reached my normal state, I discovered that I was half-famished with hunger;[1] so making a hasty toilet,[2] I went into the other room.

I found supper already laid out. My host, who stood on one side of the
50 great fireplace, leaning against the stone-work, made a graceful wave of his hand to the table, and said: –

'I pray you, be seated and sup how you please. You will, I trust, excuse me that I do not join you; but I have dined already, and I do not sup.'[3]

• •

2 a How did the Count's hand feel to the touch?

   b What did Jonathan think after shaking the Count's hand?

   c What was the bedroom like? How did Jonathan feel when he saw it?

   d What excuse did the Count find for not eating?

1 **half-famished with hunger** : very hungry.

2 **hasty toilet** : quick wash.

3 **sup** : have supper.

Dracula

3 Go on reading and complete the following table about the Count's physical appearance.

face	
nose	
forehead	
hair	
eyebrows	
mouth	
teeth	
ears	
chin	
cheeks	
hands	
nails	

• •

(...)

The Count himself came forward and took off the cover of a dish, and I fell to [1] at once on an excellent roast chicken. This, with some cheese and a salad and a bottle of old Tokay, of which I had two glasses, was my supper. During the time I was eating it the Count asked me many questions as to my journey, and I told him by degrees all I had experienced.

By this time I had finished my supper, and by my host's desire had drawn up a chair by the fire and begun to smoke a cigar which he offered me, at the same time excusing himself that he did not smoke. I had now an opportunity of observing him, and found him of a very marked physiognomy. [2]

His face was a strong – a very strong – aquiline, with high bridge of the thin nose and peculiarly arched nostrils; with lofty domed forehead, and hair

1 **fell to** : started.   2 **physiognomy** : [fɪziɒnəmi].

11

growing scantily [1] round the temples, but profusely elsewhere. His eyebrows were very massive, almost meeting over the nose, and with bushy hair that seemed to curl in its own profusion. The mouth, so far as I could see it under the heavy moustache, was fixed and rather cruel-looking, with peculiarly
70 sharp white teeth; these protruded over the lips, whose remarkable ruddiness [2] showed astonishing vitality in a man of his years. For the rest, his ears were pale and at the tops extremely pointed; the chin was broad and strong, and the cheeks firm though thin. The general effect was one of extraordinary pallor.
75 Hitherto [3] I had noticed the backs [4] of his hands as they lay on his knees in the firelight, and they had seemed rather white and fine; but seeing them now close to me, I could not but notice that they were rather coarse [5] – broad, with squat [6] fingers. Strange to say, there were hairs in the centre of the palm. The nails were long and fine, and cut to a sharp point. As the Count leaned [7]
80 over me and his hands touched me, I could not repress a shudder. It may have been that his breath was rank, [8] but a horrible feeling of nausea came over me, which, do what I would, I could not conceal. [9] The Count, evidently noticing it, drew back; and with a grim sort of smile, which showed more than he had yet done of his protuberant teeth, sat himself down again on his
85 own side of the fireplace.

• •

EXTRACT TWO

From Jonathan Harker's Journal, Chapter 2.

Read Extract 2 and complete the table that follows it.

1	**scantily** : thinly.	6	**squat** [skwɒt] : short and fat.
2	**ruddiness** : red colour.	7	**leaned** : bent.
3	**Hitherto** [hiðətuː] : Up to this time.	8	**rank** : unpleasantly stale and strong.
4	**backs** : back part.	9	**conceal** : hide.
5	**coarse** [kɔːs] : rough, unrefined.		

8 May. – I only slept a few hours when I went to bed, and feeling that I could not sleep any more, got up. I had hung my shaving-glass by the window, and was just beginning to shave. Suddenly I felt a hand on my shoulder, and heard the Count's voice saying to me, 'Good morning.' I started,[1] for it amazed me that I had not seen him, since the reflection of the glass covered the whole room behind me. In starting I had cut myself slightly, but did not notice it at the moment. Having answered the Count's salutation, I turned to the glass again to see how I had been mistaken. This time there could be no error, for the man was close to me, and I could see him over my shoulder. But there was no reflection of him in the mirror! The whole room behind me was displayed; but there was no sign of a man in it, except myself. This was startling,[2] and, coming on the top of so many strange things, was beginning to increase that vague feeling of uneasiness which I always have when the Count is near; but at that instant I saw that the cut had bled[3] a little, and the blood was trickling over my chin. I laid down the razor, turning as I did so half-round to look for some sticking-plaster. When the Count saw my face, his eyes blazed[4] with a sort of demoniac fury, and he suddenly made a grab at[5] my throat. I drew away, and his hand touched the string of beads which held the crucifix. It made an instant change in him, for the fury passed so quickly that I could hardly believe that it was ever there.

'Take care,' he said, 'take care how you cut yourself. It is more dangerous than you think in this country.' Then seizing[6] the shaving-glass, he went on: 'And this is the wretched[7] thing that has done the mischief.[8] It is a foul bauble[9] of man's vanity. Away with it!' and opening the heavy window with one wrench[10] of his terrible hand, he flung out[11] the glass, which was shattered[12] into a thousand pieces on the stones of the courtyard far below.

1	**started** : jumped because of fright and surprise.	7	**wretched** [retʃɪd] : bad.
2	**startling** : surprising, shocking.	8	**mischief** [mɪstʃɪf] : damage, harm.
3	**bled** : lost blood.	9	**bauble** : ornament of little value.
4	**blazed** : burnt brightly.	10	**wrench** : violent pull.
5	**made a grab at** : tried to take hold of.	11	**flung out** : threw out with great force.
6	**seizing** [siːzɪŋ] : taking hold of, grabbing.	12	**shattered** : broken.

1		
What Jonathan began to do after getting up		
What Jonathan suddenly felt on his shoulder		
What surprised Jonathan while looking in the mirror	.	
How the Count reacted when he saw Jonathan's blood		

Jonathan finds out that the Count is a vampire and experiences many horrors at the castle.

EXTRACT THREE

From Jonathan Harker's Journal, Chapter 3.

Focus on Similes

A simile is a figure of speech in which one thing is compared to another by the use of indicators (like or as).

e.g. He is as strong as a horse.

Three distinguishing elements can be identified in a simile:

Tenor	the first thing that is compared
Vehicle	the second thing that is compared
Ground	the link between the two things in the comparison

The Ground is rarely included in a simile, because the writer wants the reader to deduce it.

e.g.

He   is like a bull in a china shop

⇩   ⇩

TENOR   ⇨   **VEHICLE**

GROUND   because he is very clumsy

Dracula

A Useful Table

You may use the following table whenever you want to analyse a simile.

Tenor	
Vehicle	
Ground	
Effect	

1 Listen to the first part of Extract 3 and underline the two similes that Jonathan uses to describe

- the Count's coat
- the movement of the Count's fingers and toes

Now copy the above table in your exercise book twice. Then fill in the tables with the two similes you have found.

Read the text to check your answers.

• •

 I drew back behind the stonework, and looked carefully out.

What I saw was the Count's head coming out from the window. I did not see the face, but I knew the man by the neck and the movement of his back and arms. In any case, I could not mistake the hands which I had had so many opportunities of studying. I was at first interested and somewhat   5 amused, for it is wonderful how small a matter will interest and amuse a man when he is a prisoner. But my very feelings changed to repulsion and terror when I saw the whole man slowly emerge from the window and begin to crawl [1] down the castle wall over that dreadful abyss, *face down*, with his cloak spreading out around him like great wings. At first I could not believe   10 my eyes. I thought it was some trick of the moonlight, some weird [2] effect of shadow; but I kept looking, and it could be no delusion. I saw the fingers and toes grasp the corners of the stones, worn clear of the mortar [3] by the stress of

---

1   **crawl** : move slowly on hands and knees.

2   **weird** [wɪəd] : strange.

3   **mortar** : mixture of cement, sand and water used to hold bricks in place.

years, and by thus using every projection and inequality move downwards
15 with considerable speed, just as a lizard moves along a wall.

What manner of man is this, or what manner of creature is it in the
semblance of man? I feel the dread of this horrible place overpowering me; I
am in fear – in awful fear – and there is no escape for me; I am encompassed [1]
about with terrors that I dare not think of ...

● ●

2 The final part of the passage is centred on Jonathan's fear. What scares Jonathan most of all about the Count?

3 Read the first section of Extract 3 again and find a suitable title for it.

4 Listen to the next part of the Extract and answer the following questions.

   a Why did Jonathan think he was dreaming when he saw the three women?

   b What physical qualities made two of the women look like the Count?

   c What physical quality did the three of them share?

   d What made Jonathan feel uneasy?

   e What did the three women do?

Read the text to check your answers.

● ●

The Morning of 16 May

20   I suppose I must have fallen asleep; I hope so, but I fear, for all that
followed was startlingly real – so real that now, sitting here in the broad, full
sunlight of the morning, I cannot in the least believe that it was all sleep.

I was not alone. The room was the same, unchanged in any way since I
came into it; I could see along the floor, in the brilliant moonlight, my own
25 footsteps marked where I had disturbed the long accumulation of dust. In the
moonlight opposite me were three young women, ladies by their dress and
manner. I thought at the time that I must be dreaming when I saw them, for,
though the moonlight was behind them, they threw no shadow on the floor.

1   **encompassed** : surrounded.

Dracula

They came close to me and looked at me for some time and then whispered
together. Two were dark, and had high aquiline noses, like the Count's, and 30
great dark, piercing[1] eyes, that seemed to be almost red when contrasted
with the pale yellow moon. The other was fair, as fair can be, with great,
wavy masses of golden hair and eyes like pale sapphires.[2] I seemed
somehow to know her face, and to know it in connection with some dreamy
fear, but I could not recollect[3] at the moment how or where. All three had 35
brilliant white teeth, that shone like pearls against the ruby of their
voluptuous lips. There was something about them that made me uneasy,
some longing[4] and at the same time some deadly[5] fear. I felt in my heart a
wicked, burning desire that they would kiss me with those red lips. It is not
good to note this down, lest[6] some day it should meet Mina's eyes and cause 40
her pain; but it is the truth. They whispered together, and then they all three
laughed – such a silvery, musical laugh, but as hard as though the sound
never could have come through the softness of human lips. It was like the
intolerable, tingling[7] sweetness of water-glasses when played on by a
cunning[8] hand. 45

• •

5 Try to predict what will happen next.

1	**piercing** [pɪəsɪŋ] : penetrating, looking intensely and intently.	5	**deadly** : mortal.
		6	**lest** : for fear that.
2	**sapphires** : clear, bright blue precious stones.	7	**tingling** : causing a prickling sensation.
3	**recollect** : remember.	8	**cunning** : clever.
4	**longing** : desire.		

EXTRACT FOUR

From Jonathan Harker's Journal, Chapter 3.

Focus on Contrasts

1 The next section that you are going to read is full of contrasts.

Work with a partner and look for contrasting words/expressions and then complete the following chart. (Some words have already been written for you.)

WORDS/EXPRESSIONS ASSOCIATED WITH			
Lines	Pleasure	Lines	Disgust/Fear
6	delightful anticipation	6	agony
8		10	
13		14	repulsive
15-16		16	
24	languorous ecstasy	25	

• •

The fair girl shook her head coquettishly,[1] and the other two urged her on.[2] One said: –

'Go on! You are first, and we shall follow; yours is the right to begin.' The other added: –

5   'He is young and strong; there are kisses for us all.' I lay quiet, looking out under my eyelashes in an agony of delightful anticipation. The fair girl advanced and bent over me till I could feel the movement of her breath upon me. Sweet it was in one sense, honey-sweet, and sent the same tingling through the nerves as her voice, but with a bitter underlying the sweet, a

10   bitter offensiveness, as one smells in blood.

---

1 **coquettishly** [kɒketɪʃli] : in a flirting   2 **urged her on** : encouraged her.
   manner.

Dracula

I was afraid to raise my eyelids, but looked out and saw perfectly under the lashes. The fair girl went on her knees and bent over me, fairly gloating.[1] There was a deliberate voluptuousness which was both thrilling and repulsive, and as she arched[2] her neck she actually licked her lips like an animal, till I could see in the moonlight the moisture shining on the scarlet   15 lips and on the red tongue as it lapped[3] the white sharp teeth. Lower and lower went her head as the lips went below the range of my mouth and chin and seemed about to fasten on my throat. Then she paused, and I could hear the churning[4] sound of her tongue as it licked her teeth and lips, and could feel the hot breath on my neck. Then the skin of my throat began to tingle as   20 one's flesh does when the hand that is to tickle[5] it approaches nearer – nearer. I could feel the soft, shivering touch of the lips on the supersensitive skin of my throat, and the hard dents of two sharp teeth, just touching and pausing there. I closed my eyes in a languorous ecstasy and waited – waited with beating heart.   25

• •

Read to the end of the Extract and then do the activities which follow.

• •

But at that instant another sensation swept through me as quick as lightning. I was conscious of the presence of the Count, and of his being as if lapped in a storm of fury. As my eyes opened involuntarily I saw his strong hand grasp the slender[6] neck of the fair woman and with giant's power draw it back, the blue eyes transformed with fury, the white teeth champing[7] with   30 rage, and the fair cheeks blazing red with passion. But the Count! Never did I imagine such wrath[8] and fury, even in the demons of the pit.[9]

1   **gloating** : looking with wicked pleasure.
2   **arched** [ɑːtʃt] : bent to form a curve.
3   **lapped** : licked.
4   **churning** [tʃɜːnɪŋ] : violently moving.

5   **tickle** : touch a sensitive part of the body lightly, often to make someone laugh.
6   **slender** : slim.
7   **champing** : chewing noisily.
8   **wrath** [rɒθ]: violent anger.
9   **pit** : hell.

Bram Stoker

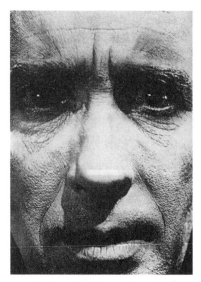

Christopher Lee as 'Dracula'.

His eyes were positively blazing. The red light in them was lurid, as if the flames of hell-fire blazed behind them. His face was deathly pale, and the
35   lines of it were hard like drawn wires; the thick eyebrows that met over the nose now seemed like a heaving bar of white-hot metal. With a fierce sweep [1] of his arm, he hurled [2] the woman from him, and then motioned to the others, as though he were beating them back; it was the same imperious gesture that I had seen used to the wolves. In a voice which, though low and almost a
40   whisper, seemed to cut through the air and then ring round the room, he exclaimed: –

'How dare you touch him, any of you? How dare you cast eyes on him when I had forbidden it? Back, I tell you all! This man belongs to me! Beware how you meddle [3] with him, or you'll have to deal with me.' The fair girl,
45   with a laugh of ribald [4] coquetry, turned to answer him: –

'You yourself never loved; you never love!' On this the other women joined, and such a mirthless, [5] hard, soulless laughter rang through the room that it almost made me faint to hear; it seemed like the pleasure of fiends. [6] Then the Count turned, after looking at my face attentively, and said in a soft whisper: –
50   'Yes, I too can love; you yourselves can tell it from the past. Is it not so?

1	**sweep** : sudden movement.	4	**ribald** : obscene but humorous.
2	**hurled** : violently threw.	5	**mirthless** [mɜːθləs] : joyless.
3	**meddle** : interfere.	6	**fiends** [fiːndz] : devils.

Dracula

Well, now I promise you that when I am done with him,[1] you shall kiss him at your will. Now go! go! I must awaken him, for there is work to be done.'

'Are we to have nothing to-night?' said one of them, with a low laugh, as she pointed to the bag which he had thrown upon the floor, and which moved as though there were some living thing within it. For answer he nodded his head. One of the women jumped forward and opened it. If my ears did not deceive me there was a gasp [2] and a low wail,[3] as of a half-smothered [4] child. The women closed round, whilst I was aghast with horror; but as I looked they disappeared, and with them the dreadful bag. There was no door near them, and they could not have passed me without my noticing. They simply seemed to fade into the rays of the moonlight and pass out through the window, for I could see outside the dim, shadowy forms for a moment before they entirely faded away.

Then the horror overcame me, and I sank down unconscious.

• •

2 a Fill in this Chart about the Count's facial features.

eyes	
face	
the lines of his face	
eyebrows	

b Explain why:
- in your opinion the Count was accused of being unable to love.
- the Count stopped the three women.
- the Count gave the three women the "bag".
- Jonathan sank into unconsciousness.

---

1 **when I am done with him** : when I've finished with him.

2 **gasp** : sound made by sudden breathing.

3 **wail** : sorrowful cry.

4 **smothered** : suffocated.

Bram Stoker

c Look at the adjectives below and select the ones that you would use to describe Jonathan's attitude/feelings in the Extract. Compare your choices with your classmates.

> longing   dreamy   condescending   unconscious
> wise   bored   irritated   polite   sweet   intolerable
> voluptuous   attentive   sleepy   horrified   mirthless
> conscious   absent-minded

Focus on Similes

3 a Look for the similes used in the Extract from lines 26-64 and complete the following table.

Line	Simile

b Compare what you have written with your classmates and then decide whether the similes:

- slow down the pace of narration
- quicken the pace of narration
- increase the nightmarish atmosphere
- awaken horror in the reader

Discuss your choices in class.

> Jonathan begins to explore the castle during the daytime. He discovers the Count asleep in one of fifty boxes of earth in a chapel.

Dracula

EXTRACT FIVE

From Jonathan Harker's Journal, Chapter 4.

1 Listen to the following Extract and say:

- who Jonathan was looking for ....
- why Jonathan had to search the Count's body ....
- how Jonathan felt when he opened the box ....

Read the text to check your answers.

• •

30 June, morning

I went through the door in the corner and down the winding stair and along the dark passage to the old chapel. I knew now well enough where to find the monster I sought.

The great box was in the same place, close against the wall, but the lid [1] was laid on it, not fastened down, but with the nails ready in their places to   5 be hammered home. [2] I knew I must search the body for the key, so I raised the lid and laid it back against the wall; and then I saw something which filled my very soul with horror.

• •

2 Work with a partner and match the words below with their definitions.

trickled	gorged	swollen	pouches
bloated	gash	repletion	leech

a completely filled	**b** swollen
c flowed in a thin stream	**d** become larger in volume
e areas of baggy skin under the eyes	**f** small blood-sucking worm
g deep cut, wound	**h** state of being completely filled

Compare your choices with your classmates.

Then read the following passage and underline the words you have just defined.

---

1   **lid** : cover.   2   **hammered home** : hit into position with a hammer.

Bram Stoker

Continue listening and do the activities which follow.

• •

There lay the Count, but looking as if his youth had been half-renewed,
10 for the white hair and moustache were changed to dark iron-grey; the cheeks
were fuller, and the white skin seemed ruby-red underneath; the mouth was
redder than ever, for on the lips were gouts ¹ of fresh blood, which trickled
from the corners of the mouth and ran over the chin and neck. Even the deep,
burning eyes seemed set amongst swollen flesh, for the lids and pouches
15 underneath were bloated. It seemed as if the whole awful creature were
simply gorged with blood; he lay like a filthy ² leech, exhausted with his
repletion. I shuddered as I bent over to touch him, and every sense in me
revolted at the contact; but I had to search, or I was lost.

(…)

20 I felt all over the body, but no sign could I find of the key. Then I stopped
and looked at the Count. There was a mocking smile on the bloated face which
seemed to drive me mad. This was the being I was helping to transfer to
London, where, perhaps for centuries to come, he might, amongst its teeming ³
millions, satiate his lust ⁴ for blood, and create a new and ever widening circle
25 of semi-demons to batten on ⁵ the helpless. The very thought drove me mad. A
terrible desire came upon me to rid the world of such a monster. There was no
lethal weapon at hand, but I seized a shovel ⁶ which the workmen had been
using to fill the cases, and lifting it high, struck, with the edge downward, at
the hateful face. But as I did so the head turned, and the eyes fell full upon me,
30 with all their blaze of basilisk ⁷ horror. The sight seemed to paralyse me, and
the shovel turned in my hand and glanced ⁸ from the face, merely making a
deep gash above the forehead. The shovel fell from my hand across the box,
and as I pulled it away the flange ⁹ of the blade caught the edge of the lid,
which fell over again, and hid the horrid thing from my sight. The last glimpse

1   **gouts** [gaʊts] : *(here)* drops.
2   **filthy** : very dirty.
3   **teeming** : *(here)* a great many.
4   **lust** : desire, wish.
5   **batten on** : torment.

6   **shovel** : tool like a spade, with a short handle.
7   **basilisk** : *(here)* malicious.
8   **glanced** : *(here)* hit at an angle and moved away.
9   **flange** : *(here)* edge.

Dracula

I had was of the bloated face, bloodstained and fixed with a grin of malice   35
which would have held its own in the nethermost[1] hell.

I thought and thought what should be my next move, but my brain
seemed on fire, and I waited with a despairing feeling growing over me.

• •

3 a While listening, focus on the way in which Jonathan describes the Count and
complete the following phrases:

1 The white hair and moustache were changed to ....

2 .... fuller.

3 The white skin seemed .... underneath.

4 .... redder.

5 On the lips .... of fresh blood.

6 ....of the eyes were bloated.

7 It seemed as if the whole awful creature were simply .... blood.

Read the text to check your answers.

b Which animal is the Count compared to? Why do you think such an animal has
been chosen?

A Chain of Actions and Reactions

4 Complete the following sentences.

a Jonathan's actions/reactions at seeing the Count:

1 When Jonathan tried to touch the Count, he ....

2 On touching the Count every sense ....

3 The Count's bloated face seemed to ....

4 Jonathan seized a .... , lifted it and .... the
Count's face.

1   **nethermost** : lowest.

b The Count's reactions while Jonathan was about to strike him:

   1 His head ....

   2 His eyes .... upon Jonathan with ....

c Jonathan's reactions at being looked at by the Count:

   1 The sight of the Count seemed to ....

   2 The shovel .... in his hand and .... from the face, ... a deep gash above the ....

   3 The shovel .... from Jonathan's hand.

5 Would you react in a similar way if you were in Jonathan's place? Why/why not?

A Closer Look at Facial Features

6 a Which adjectives are commonly used to describe facial features?

  b Match the facial parts in the box below with their corresponding adjectives.

| chin | eyebrows | nose | cheeks |
| forehead | eyes | lips | mouth |

double, pointed   ....

thick, cherry   ....

high   ....

piercing, hazel   ....

bushy   ....

rosy, plump   ....

wide, mean   ....

aquiline, hook   ....

Compare your answers with your classmates.

  c • What thought/s seemed to drive Jonathan mad?

     • Why couldn't Jonathan concentrate at the end of the Extract?

Dracula

Jonathan's Feelings

7 Work with a partner and select the adjective/s which best describe/s Jonathan's feelings at the end of the Extract.

☐ rash   ☐ disconsolate   ☐ frantic   ☐ worried

☐ miserable   ☐ sad   ☐ disheartened   ☐ frenzied

Use your monolingual dictionary to look up the meaning of the words you don't know!

The Count manages to arrive in England. Jonathan's fiancée Mina is worried and goes to a hospital in Buda-Pesth, where Jonathan has been ill. They get married and return to England. Some time later the Count turns his attention to Mina, appears to her and makes her drink his blood. She will now become a vampire herself unless Dracula is killed.

The group of vampire hunters, which includes Jonathan and Mina, finds and neutralises forty-nine of the fifty boxes of earth. In the meantime the Count arranges for his return to Transylvania in the last box. The Count is pursued and will eventually die.

8 a How do you think the Count will die?

  b What do you expect will happen to his body after his death?

EXTRACT SIX

From Mina Harker's Journal, Chapter 27.

1 Listen to the following Extract taken from the end of the book and write notes about:

The setting at the beginning of the passage	
The Count's appearance	
What was used to kill the Count	
What happened to the Count's body	
What the Count's face looked like at the moment of final dissolution	
The setting at the end of the passage	

Bram Stoker

 The sun was almost down on the mountain tops, and the shadows of the whole group fell long upon the snow. I saw the Count lying within the box upon the earth, some of which the rude [1] falling from the cart had scattered over him. He was deathly pale, just like a waxen image, and the red eyes
5 glared with the horrible vindictive look which I knew too well.

As I looked, the eyes saw the sinking sun, and the look of hate in them turned to triumph.

But, on the instant, came the sweep and flash of Jonathan's great knife. I shrieked [2] as I saw it shear [3] through the throat; whilst at the same moment
10 Mr Morris's bowie knife [4] plunged in the heart.

It was like a miracle; but before our very eyes, and almost in the drawing of a breath, the whole body crumbled [5] into dust and passed from our sight.

I shall be glad as long as I live that even in that moment of final dissolution there was in the face a look of peace, such as I never could have
15 imagined might have rested there.

The Castle of Dracula now stood out against the red sky, and every stone of its broken battlements [6] was articulated against the light of the setting sun.

1 **rude** : sudden, violent.

2 **shrieked** [ʃriːkt] : screamed, cried.

3 **shear** : cut.

4 **bowie knife** : long knife with a blade double-edged at the point.

5 **crumbled** : broke into small pieces and dissolved itself.

6 **battlements** : walls.

Dracula

Focus on Narration/Narrators

1 Tick appropriately:

a The story is told by:

☐ one narrator

☐ different narrators

b The story is told using:

☐ the first person

☐ the third person

c The main narrator/s refer/s to himself/herself/themselves using:

☐ the third person

☐ the first person

d The main narrator is:

☐ within the story and at its centre

☐ outside the story

☐ within the story but not at its centre

2 It should be clear now that *Dracula* is an example of first person narrative and that the author decided to use more than one narrator to tell the story in the form of Journals. Why do you think that the writer made such a choice?

☐ to puzzle the reader

☐ to offer different viewpoints

☐ to create more suspense by shifting from one narrator to the other

☐ to contrast the different characters

Compare your choices with your classmates.

Summing up

3 Write down a few lines on what you have learnt about vampires.

4 Write a summary of the Extracts you have read, using appropriate linkers and your own words.

5 A FILM VERSION

Imagine that you are a film director and that you are asked to transpose the story into a film which should be an alternative to the already existing ones. Work in a group and decide:

- whether your film is going to be in black and white or colour.
- where to set the story.
- what costumes you are going to use.
- the perspective you would choose to narrate the story.
- how to visualise "horror".

6 Word-File

Revise all the new words you have met throughout the Extracts you have just read: highlight the words which you think will be useful for communication and insert them in the following table.

Useful Words	Meaning

CROSS-CURRICULAR DATA

The Gothic Story

The term 'Gothic' has been established as the name defining a sinister corner of modern Western imagination. In an architectural context it refers to a European style which flourished from the late 12th to the 15th century. In its earliest sense, the word 'Gothic' was used as an adjective denoting the language and ethnic identity of the Goths, Germanic people who moved from the Baltic Sea to the Iberian peninsula from the 3rd to the 5th century AD. By the end of the 18th century the term 'Gothic' was used to mean 'medieval' and 'barbarous'.

Horace Walpole's *The Castle of Otranto: A Gothic Story* (1764) is founded upon this usage. It denotes a tale about cruelty, brutality and superstition in the Middle Ages.

The novels of early Gothic writers are peopled by poisoners and diabolical murderers who plot against helpless maidens. Such tales show no respect for the past since they portray the former ages as prisons of delusion.

It was Edgar Allan Poe's *The Fall of the House of Usher* (1839) which introduced 'decadence', a new keynote, into Gothic fiction, through the decline and extinction of an old family line. Little by little, the Gothic tale started to combine a fearful sense of inheritance with a claustrophobic sense of enclosure in space: the combination of both dimensions produced an impression of sickening descent into disintegration.

A particular feature of Gothic fiction is the presence of old buildings: houses, castles, convents, madhouses, isolated country houses, etc. These are sites of human decay, degeneration and even decomposition. The Gothic house may be interpreted as a structure with crypts and cellars which hosts our deepest fears, including the fear of death, decay and confinement.

Perhaps the best way to sum up Gothic fiction is to quote Joyce Carol Oates in the preface to her novel *Bellefleur* (1980):

'The imaginative construction of a 'Gothic' novel involves the systematic transposition of realistic psychological and emotional experiences into 'Gothic' elements. We all experience mirrors that distort, we all age at different speeds, we have known people who want to suck our life's blood from us, like vampires; we feel haunted by the dead – if not precisely by the dead then by thoughts of them... . All these factors the novelist who wants to write an 'experimental Gothic' will transpose into Gothic terms. If Gothicism has the power to move us (and it certainly has the power to fascinate the novelist) it is only because its roots are in psychological realism.'

The Gothic Story

Outstanding Works:

The Castle of Otranto: A Gothic Story (1764) by Horace Walpole: it tells how the Prince of Otranto tries to marry his son's fiancée, after he has been killed by a mysterious plumed helmet.

The Mysteries of Udolpho (1794) by Ann Radcliffe: about an unscrupulous adventurer who forces a girl to live according to his principles.

Frankenstein (1818) by Mary Shelley: about the failure of a scientist's attempt to create the perfect being.

Dracula (1897) by Bram Stoker.

The Assignation (1988) by Joyce Carol Oates: a spine-tingling collection of tales.

Note down:

1 the earliest use of the term 'Gothic'.

2 its use by the end of the 18th century.

3 the characteristics of early Gothic novels.

4 what Poe introduced.

5 what the 'Gothic House' may represent.

6 what the Gothic novel is, according to Joyce Carol Oates.

Earthbound

by Roberta Simpson Brown

Roberta Simpson Brown

Roberta Simpson Brown graduated from Berea College in Berea, Kentucky.

She is a language arts teacher in Louisville, Kentucky (with over thirty years' experience in the classroom) and is also a performing storyteller.

Her work features original stories with contemporary settings and truly chilling endings. Many of her stories have an 'O. Henry'-like twist at the end.

She has earned the title 'Queen of the Cold-Blooded Tales'.

Main works:

The Walking Trees and other Scary Stories, including
    'Earthbound' (1991)

Scary Stories for All Ages (audiobook) (1992)

The Scariest Stories Ever (audiobook) (1992)

Queen of the Cold-Blooded Tales (1993)

Scared in School (1997)

BEFORE READING

1 Work in a group and:

   a Give a definition of the word 'horror'.

   b Mention as many 'horror characters' as you can (think of novels, television, films, etc.).

   c Try to guess which literary genre the word 'horror' comes from.

2 Turn the page upside down and read the definition of 'horror' taken from the Webster's Concise Interactive Encyclopedia.

Genre of fiction and film, devoted primarily to scaring the reader or audience, but often also aiming to be cathartic through their exaggeration of the bizarre and grotesque.

Dominant figures in the horror tradition are Mary Shelley (*Frankenstein* 1818), Edgar Allan Poe, Bram Stoker, H P Lovecraft and, among contemporary writers, Stephen King and Clive Barker.

Horror is derived from the Gothic novel, which dealt with shock effects, as well as from folk tales and ghost stories throughout the ages. Horror writing tends to use motifs such as vampirism, the eruption of ancient evil, and monstrous transformation, which often derive from folk traditions, as well as more recent concerns such as psychopathology.

3 Look at the title of the story and decide whether 'bound' is used as a verb or a noun.

Earthbound

In a group work out the possible meaning of the title and then guess what the story is about. Check your ideas while reading the story.

4 Listen to the beginning of the story and explain why Marty:

- had to leave
- came back
- walked slowly

Read the text to check your answers.

Roberta Simpson Brown

Marty got out near the church and headed down the road to the old farm he loved. He couldn't remember exactly how long he'd been away. He hadn't wanted to leave in the first place, but some things couldn't be helped. [1] He'd had no choice.

5   The worst thing about leaving was the way his mother had cried. He'd been the only one left to help her work the farm, but he hadn't been able after the accident. He wouldn't be coming back now except for his mother's grieving. [2] She hadn't actually asked him to come, but he could tell by her crying she wanted him to.

10   His legs felt wobbly [3] as he walked along because he wasn't used to walking. He had to go slowly, but he didn't mind. It gave him a chance to look at the farm. Most things hadn't changed, yet something was different. It gave Marty a peculiar feeling because he couldn't figure out [4] what it was. He felt out of place, and that disturbed him.

• •

5 Complete the following table.

Setting	
Where Marty 'got out'	
What the farm looked like when Marty came back	
What disturbed Marty	

Compare your answers with your classmates.

---

1   **helped** : (*here*) avoided.

2   **grieving** [griːvɪŋ] : suffering sadness.

3   **wobbly** : unsteady, shaky, weak after illness.

4   **figure out** : imagine, picture mentally.

36

Earthbound

6 Read Part 2 and try to guess the meaning of the words from their context. Check your definitions in your monolingual dictionary.

Word	Line	Your Guess	Dictionary Meaning
bound			
picking up			
rustle			
jarred			
barn			
looming			
combine			
roll in			

• •

He knew every inch of those corn fields, and he knew he'd always be   15
bound to that land. The wind was picking up, and he could hear the corn
rustle like corn fairies whispering. He remembered how his mother used to
read him that story by Carl Sandburg.[1]

In the farmhouse down the road, Marty's mother was thinking about the
old days, too. She was wishing this stormy night could be like those when   20
the family was together. Her husband would come in from the fields, and
they'd sit around the fire after supper and she'd read to Marty. After her
husband died, she had still had Marty, and he had been such a comfort. She
dreaded[2] stormy nights now that she was alone. This would be a bad one.
The first clap[3] of thunder had jarred Marty's picture right off the wall.   25

Back down the road, Marty tried to walk faster. He thought he'd be home
by the time the storm broke, but he was very tired now. Every breath he took
burned his lungs. His throat felt dry and dusty, and his shoes were covered
with dirt.

1   **Carl Sandburg** (1878-1967) : American   2   **dreaded** : was afraid of, feared.
    writer and poet who won Pulitzer   3   **clap** : explosive sound.
    Prizes for his book about Abraham
    Lincoln and for his poetry.

30 He could see the shape of the old barn looming in the distance now. The combine would be inside. It was odd, but he hadn't thought of it since the accident.

He saw the farmhouse beyond and wished the black clouds wouldn't roll in so fast.

35 He really needed to hurry, but his body wouldn't respond like it used to.

Detail from 'Christina's World' (1948) by Andrew Wyeth.

7 Say whether you agree or disagree with the following statements and support your choices by referring to the text.

  a Marty did not remember anything about the land.

  b It was windy.

  c Marty's mother was working in the fields.

  d Marty's father was at home.

  e Marty's mother was scared of stormy nights.

  f Marty's picture fell from the wall.

  g Marty believed he would be home before the storm broke.

  h Marty hardly breathed.

Earthbound

Focus on Similes

8 Scan Part 2 and underline the simile that the author uses to describe:

- the noise the corn makes

9 Now complete the following table.

	Simile
Tenor	
Vehicle	
Ground	
Effect	

10 Read Part 3 carefully and then fill in the following table by saying what:

troubled Marty as he passed the barn	
Marty asked himself	
Marty was looking forward to	
Marty did under the porch	
Marty's mother did when she heard the noise	
Marty did when his mother appeared at the door	

As he passed the barn, the air felt heavy and damp [1] and there was a strong musty [2] odour around him. Something definitely was not right, and it worried him.

But he was almost home. He could see the light in the window, and he
40 knew his mother would be happy to see him. He wondered if she'd think he'd changed much.

The first raindrops hit as Marty reached the yard. His energy was spent, but he forced himself to keep going. He could hardly wait to see his mother's face.

The storm began to rage [3] around him as he climbed the steps to the
45 porch. [4] The wind tore at his clothes and drove him against the railing. He stumbled [5] and grabbed [6] the old porch swing. [7] His weight banged it against the side of the house.

Marty's mother heard the noise, and through the window, Marty saw her move to the door to see what had happened. As the door opened, he turned
50 towards her and gave her his biggest smile.

• •

11 Complete the following summary (Parts 1-3). Fill in the blanks or circle the appropriate word:

Marty got out (*near/far from/inside*) the church and made .... the old barn. He could not remember (*how often/how far/how long*) he had been ....

(*Secondly/First/At first*) he had not wanted to leave, but then he had had no .... He would not be (*coming back/going/leaving*) but for his mother's ....

His (*head/arms/legs*) felt weak, as he was not used to .... A storm was .... to break.

In the (*old barn/farmhouse/fields*) his mother remembered when the family was .... before her husband's ....

Back down the road Marty (*stopped/moved/tried*) to walk faster before the storm .... In the (*distance/barn/heights*) he could see the old barn and the (*fields/swing/farmhouse*).

1	**damp** : slightly wet, moist.	5	**stumbled** : nearly fell.
2	**musty** : of a mouldy or stale smell.	6	**grabbed** : seized.
3	**rage** : be violent.	7	**swing** : a seat on ropes or chains for swinging on or in.
4	**porch** : a covered shelter for the entrance of a building.		

Earthbound

He (*asked/requested /asked himself*) whether his mother would think he had
.... much. He was looking forward to .... her face. When he
reached the porch, he (*kicked/put down/seized*) the old porch .... and
banged it against the side of the house.

His mother came (*in/to/out*) to see what (*happened/had happened/would
happen*) and Marty smiled .... her.

Prediction

12 On the basis of what you have read so far, what do you think will happen next?
Write down your personal conclusion to the story.

13 Listen to the final part of the story and write what:

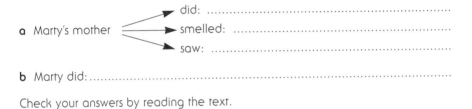

a Marty's mother → did: ....
→ smelled: ....
→ saw: ....

b Marty did: ....

Check your answers by reading the text.

. . . .

For a few seconds, she stood there blinking,[1] trying to adjust to the
darkness. She smelled a musty, rotten[2] odour, and then a flash of lightning
revealed the figure before her. In an instant, she saw the grinning[3] skull and
the rotting burial[4] clothes of her dead son. She stared in disbelief as the thing
from the grave reached out to her. Then Marty's mother fell forward into the   55
skeleton's bony arms.

. . . .

14 At the beginning of the story 'something' gives us an idea where Marty came
from. What is it?

1 **blinking** : looking with eyes opening and shutting.	3 **grinning** : smiling broadly.
2 **rotten** : unpleasant.	4 **burial** [beriəl] : of the funeral.

41

Focus on the Conclusion

15 Did you like the end of the story? Did you think it was:

- [ ] inconsistent
- [ ] unexpected
- [ ] predictable
- [ ] disappointing
- [ ] amazing
- [ ] other

Tick appropriately, then justify your choice/s.

16 Is the actual outcome different from the one you wrote?

17 Is the conclusion plausible within the framework of the story?

18 Work with a partner and try to give a definition of a 'surprise ending', then turn the page upside down to check.

In a story with a surprise ending, the writer deceives the reader by leading her/him to expect something to happen. The ending, however, is quite different to what was expected.

19 Word-File

Revise all the new words you have met throughout the story you have just read: highlight the words which you think will be useful for communication and insert them in the following table.

Useful Words	Meaning

CROSS-CURRICULAR DATA

The Horror Story

Its origins go back to the Gothic novel: Gothic writers were, in fact, the very first who discovered the charm of horror.

Edgar Allan Poe still used the conventional elements of Gothicism but also created new stories in which terror did not derive only from strange, supernatural apparitions, but mainly from the maze of the human mind and the depths of man's soul. In his work *The Imp of the Perverse* (1845) he wrote:

'We stand upon the brink of a precipice. We peer into the abyss – we grow sick and dizzy. Our first impulse is to shrink from danger. Unaccountably we remain. By slow degrees our sickness and dizziness and horror become merged in a cloud of unnameable feeling. […] But out of this our cloud upon the precipice's edge, there grows into palpability, a shape, far more terrible than any genius or any demon of a tale, and yet it is but a thought, although a fearful one, and one which chills the very marrow of our bones with the fierceness of the delight of its horror. It is merely the idea of what would be our sensations during the sweeping precipitancy of a fall from such a height. And this fall – this rushing annihilation – for the very reason that it involves that one most ghastly and loathsome of all the most loathsome and ghastly images of death and suffering which have ever presented themselves to our imagination – for this very cause do we now the most vividly desire it. And because our reason violently deters us from the brink, therefore do we the most impetuously approach it.'

Common Characteristics of Horror Stories:	
terror:	not so much of reality as of total annihilation
colours:	black, red, gold and white are dominant
enclosure:	inside a room, a building, a coffin, etc. which act as protective wombs but sometimes also become vehicles of self-destruction
descent:	into something which symbolises probing into the unconscious
nightmares:	terror and horror do not originate from the normality of the external world but from the abnormality of the characters' inner selves.

The Horror Story

It should now be clear why horror writing tends to use themes such as vampirism, the eruption of ancient evil and monstrous transformation, which often derive from folk traditions. To this framework, some modern horror stories add elements of terror in the form of supernatural entities (aliens, x-file creatures, possessed people, machinery, etc.) which act with malevolence for different purposes.

In his Foreword to his book *Night Shift* (1977), Stephen King wrote:

'When you read horror, you don't really believe what you read. You don't believe in vampires, werewolves, trucks that suddenly start up and drive themselves. The horrors that we all do believe in are…: hate, alienation, growing lovelessly old, tottering out into a hostile world on the unsteady legs of adolescence… The tale of monstrosity and terror is a basket loosely packed with phobias; when the writer passes by, you take one of his imaginary horrors out of the basket and put one of your real ones in – at least for a time.'

Outstanding Works:

MS Found in a Bottle (1833) by Edgar Allan Poe: in which the narrator himself is about to be sucked into a whirpool.

The Masque of the Red Death (1842) by Edgar Allan Poe: about a Prince and his courtiers who die struck down by the monstrous Red Death (the plague).

The Pit and the Pendulum (1843) by Edgar Allan Poe: about how men were punished if their religious beliefs did not agree with the beliefs of the church.

Dracula (1897) by Bram Stoker: the terrifying story of the famous Transylvanian vampire.

Note down:

1 the origins of Edgar Allan Poe's horror.

2 why 'the fall' is desirable, according to Poe.

3 what happens when we read about a writer's imaginary horrors, according to Stephen King.

Carlotta

by Adèle Geras

Adèle Geras

Adèle Geras was born in 1944 in Jerusalem. She was educated in England at Roedean School, Brighton. Later she attended St. Hilda's College, Oxford, where she obtained a B. A. in French and Spanish.

During her time at Oxford she appeared at the Comedy Theatre and after Oxford she went on to the Fortune Theatre as a professional singer.

She taught French for three years in Droylesden, Lancashire.

Her travels have taken her to Borneo, Nigeria, Gambia, Tanzania and Israel.

She is married with two daughters and now lives in Manchester.

Main works:

The Girls in the Velvet Frame (1979)

Apricots at Midnight (1982)

Voyage (1983)

Happy Endings (1991)

Watching the Roses (1992)

From Lullaby to Lullaby (1997)

BEFORE READING

Focus on the Title of a Story

1 In every story the title may:

- arouse expectation in the reader
- give an idea about the plot of the story
- refer to the main character/theme of the story
- say something about the way in which the story is narrated

Look at the title and subtitle of this story:

Carlotta

Diary of Edward Stonely, submitted in evidence at the Coroner's Inquest, 15 May 1993

Point out the function/s that you think they fulfil. Read the story and see if you were right.

2 You are going to read a ghost story. Work with a partner and define:

- a ghost
- a ghost story

3 Why do you think that ghosts come back to the world of the living?

4 Read the beginning of the story and fill in the following table which refers to the narrator.

What the doctor suggested	
Marital status	
Age	
Occupation	
What he wishes	
Who he feels like	

My doctor (I refuse to call him 'my shrink',[1] although that's what he is. It seems like an admission of madness.) has said that the dreams might stop altogether if I write everything down. It would be, he suggested, a kind of purging.[2] It would clear my system of what he calls 'unresolved guilts.'[3]

5   I felt a fool consulting him in the first place, but my dreams were becoming so dreadful that I was deliberately keeping myself awake for as long as I could every night. This meant that I was irritable and moody at school, tearing strips off[4] both pupils and colleagues for no good reason. I was also horrible at home, to my wife Annie, whom I love more than anyone

10 except my little daughter, Beth. I had not yet reached the point of taking my moods out on a four year old, but I can't have been the pleasantest dad in the world. The worst of it was, however hard I tried to stay awake, my eyelids closed in the end. They always did, every night, and every night, there she was: Carlotta.

15   'Start at the beginning,' Dr Armstrong said when I made some remark about not knowing where to begin. 'Don't leave anything out. Go on to the end of what you have to say and then stop. Write it as a kind of diary, whenever you feel you have something to say.' He made it sound so easy. Here goes:

19 November 1992

20   My name is Edward Stonely. I am thirty years old. I teach Art at St Peter's School in the small town of W... . I'd rather not name it. I am good at what I do. I enjoy the teaching. When I left Art School, I had the mad idea that I might make a living from painting and sculpture, and took the job at the

25 school just to make ends meet[5] till I hit the big time.[6]

   That was seven years ago. The big time isn't something I think about any more, not really, though I do sometimes wish I had more time to give to my own work. As it is, I paint and sculpt mostly during the school holidays, and I'm happy to do so, because of Annie and Beth. I would be happy to do

30 almost anything for them, in spite of everything. It's because I don't want to

---

1 **shrink** : (slang) a psychiatrist (from 'head-shrinker').

2 **purging** : physical and spiritual cleaning.

3 **guilts** : mental obsessions with the idea of having done wrong.

4 **tearing strips off** : angrily rebuking.

5 **to make ends meet** : to manage financially.

6 **hit the big time** : became rich and famous.

hurt them that I'm writing all this down, trying to get myself sorted out [1] before it's too late.

I have a good job, a lovely wife and child, a house I can afford to pay for, a reasonable future. You would think, wouldn't you, that there was nothing left to wish for, but there is. I wish for peace. I wish I could be rid of Carlotta.   35
There. I've written it down, so now maybe the blackness and solidity of the words will be like a magic spell to wipe my mind clean of those terrible dreams. I feel like Hamlet. I suppose you would say I identify with him, because of what happened to Carlotta, but we studied the play at school and I remember one quotation from it very well because I've thought it myself   40
many times over the past few weeks. 'O God,' Hamlet says, 'I could be bounded in a nutshell and count myself a king of infinite space, were it not that I have bad dreams.' That's exactly what I think.

• •

5 Read Part 2 carefully and look out for details about:

- the love story between Edward and Carlotta.
- the way in which Carlotta dies.

Discuss what you have found out in a group.

• •

22 November

I can see it's pointless going any further without writing about Carlotta. I   45
was in love with her for a year when I was seventeen, and she a little younger. She turned up at school one September, out of the blue, [2] and the minute I saw her I knew she was different.

Plenty of other girls in the class were pretty, and I'd had my flirtations with quite a lot of them, kissing in the dark at the movies, or at discos, or   50
parties, sighing a bit but not really suffering when the relationships came to a natural end. Good teenage fun. From the moment Carlotta arrived at school,

1 **get myself sorted out** : solve my problems.

2 **out of the blue** : unexpectedly, suddenly.

everything altered for me. The other lads [1] didn't rate [2] her at all, so there wasn't much competition for her favours.

55 'Funny-looking,' my friend Geoff called her.

'Flat as a pancake,' said Marty, the class sexist pig.

'Silent, too,' said Pete, and their attitudes summed up what everyone thought about Carlotta except me. I could see that her thin body, and her strange, widely-spaced yellowy-green eyes in a somewhat flat face were not 60 conventionally pretty, but they made my mouth dry whenever I looked at her; and my heart pounded [3] when I passed close to her and smelled the wonderful fragrance that seemed to float about her hair.

Her hair ... even Geoff and Marty and Pete agreed they had never seen anything like it. She wore it long and loose [4] around her shoulders, and it 65 waved and moved as she walked with a life of its own. Everyone called it black, but that was taking the easy way out. I spent hours staring at it, and there were blues and greens and even reds mixed up in the colour somehow, and a gleam [5] on it as it caught the light.

Detail from 'Am Bauch liegender weiblicher Akt'
(1917) by Egon Schiele.

1	**lads** : boys.	4	**loose** : not held together.
2	**rate** : take into consideration.	5	**gleam** : reflection of light.
3	**pounded** : beat heavily.		

Carlotta

I spent two weeks watching her at the beginning of that term, and then I could bear it no longer. Looking back, I can see that even the way our relationship started was odd. There was no leading up to it, no flirtation, no 'my friend fancies your friend' kind of negotiation that goes on in school romances.

We were in the Art Room, clearing up. There was no one else there. She was washing brushes in the sink. I came up behind her and buried[1] my face in her hair. For a moment it felt as though I were drowning in the fragrance and the softness, and I prayed that I would never ever need to come up for air. She trembled, and then turned to face me.

Have you ever seen dry paper and wood flare up[2] when you drop a lighted match on them? That's what happened to us. To Carlotta and me. Love had set us alight[3] and we caught fire. We crackled[4] and burned and leapt up in blinding[5] flames of scarlet and gold. We were consumed.

For six months, everything seemed to disappear, and there were just the two of us and our passion in the whole world. And then (like a fire) the love on my part began to flicker a little, and dwindle[6] and die. I'm not making excuses for myself. I know what I did was probably harsher[7] than it need have been, but how was I to know that Carlotta would react as she did? I came to the conclusion that our relationship had to end, and I told her so. It happens all the time, doesn't it? Well, doesn't it? Don't boys and girls split up every day of the week with no harm[8] done?

Carlotta seemed very calm when I told her. The yellow eyes widened. Her face turned quite white. She said a strange thing, one whose meaning I am only now beginning to understand:

'I'm not ready to let you go. Not yet. Not ever.'

Then she turned and left the room and that was the last time anyone saw her alive.

No one had an explanation for how she came to fall off the bridge over the rain-swollen[9] river; with nobody seeing her; nor for why she should have died when we all knew she was a strong swimmer. One theory was that her hair had become entangled on some underwater obstacle as she fell, and that

1	**buried** : placed, hid.	6	**dwindle** : lose importance, decline.
2	**flare up** : burst into flame.	7	**harsher** : more severe, crueller.
3	**set us alight** : set us on fire.	8	**harm** : hurt, damage.
4	**crackled** : made a repeated slight cracking sound.	9	**rain-swollen** : fuller because of the rain.
5	**blinding** : very bright.		

she was unable to free herself. No one else knew that I had ditched her [1] hours before 'the accident'. No one else knew that Carlotta meant to die. Me and Hamlet. Neither of us guessed that love could be so strong, so unforgiving.

John Everett Millais, 'Ophélie' (1852).

Focus on Carlotta

6 Look for details which refer to Carlotta's appearance and fill in the following Character-Chart:

Body	
Eyes	
Face	
Hair	

7 Which physical characteristics are given more relevance? Why?

8 What does the phrase 'flat as a pancake' on line 55 refer to?

---

1   **ditched her** : ended the relationship with her.

Carlotta

9 How long does the relationship between Edward and Carlotta last?

10 Why does Edward say: 'Me and Hamlet. Neither of us guessed that love could be so strong, unforgiving.'? Reading the information below might be helpful!

> In Shakespeare's tragedy, Hamlet is haunted by his father's ghost who demands revenge against his brother Claudius, who killed him. To observe his uncle's behaviour Hamlet pretends to be mad and even treats his fiancèe Ophelia badly. He involuntarily kills her father Polonius and drives Ophelia to madness, too. She commits suicide and Hamlet feels responsible for her death.

11 Read Part 3 and note:

a what happens to Edward after Carlotta's death.

b how Carlotta haunts Edward.

c Dr Armstrong's suggestions.

d how Edward's attitude to Carlotta's ghost gradually changes.

• •

29 November   105

I grieved [1] for Carlotta. Of course I did. I was genuinely sorry that she was dead. Of course I was, but I have to admit that a tiny part of me was furious with her. I can see, I said to myself, what she is saying: 'You killed me, Edward. You did. So suffer.' And I did suffer a bit, but I got over it. I went to Art School. I met Annie. We fell in love and married. Beth was born. I hardly   110 ever thought about Carlotta. Then a few months ago, the dreams started. Dr Armstrong said:

'Tell me what happens in these dreams. Why they are so dreadful. [2]

'They don't sound dreadful when I tell them,' I said. 'It's Carlotta speaking. Just her head floating in water, with her hair drifting [3] backwards   115 and forwards like seaweed. [4] She says: I'm coming. I haven't forgotten. I'll be there soon. Very soon, and then we'll be together for ever. I shall touch you, she says and then she stretches out [5] two hands in front of her and they're all

---

1	**grieved** : felt great sadness.
2	**dreadful** : terrible, horrible.
3	**drifting** : carried by a current of water.

| 4 | **seaweed** : any large algae growing in the sea or on rocks below the high water mark. |
| 5 | **stretches out** : extends. |

120 bones and fragments of skin and I know that if I don't wake up now she will
clutch[1] me in her hideous[2] fingers.'

'Hmm,' Dr Armstrong said. 'How very unpleasant. You clearly still feel responsible for Carlotta's unfortunate accident … still perceive it as suicide. Have you tried painting a picture of her? Or perhaps making a clay[3] model … Maybe that would help … giving your nightmares a real, physical presence.'

125 I promised Dr Armstrong that I would try.

10 February 1993

I haven't written in this notebook for some weeks. I think I may be cured. I have much to be grateful to Dr Armstrong for. The dreams have almost completely left me. Just before Christmas, I started work on a series of
130 paintings I call 'Portraits of Carlotta'. Annie (who knows everything) tried to pretend she didn't mind that I was spending every moment when I was not at school 'locked up in the studio with another woman', as she put it.

All through the Christmas holidays I slaved[4] over my canvases.[5] There are enough here for an exhibition, but I am reluctant to let anyone see them.
135 Carlotta's yellow eyes follow me wherever I go. There's one portrait in particular I'm pleased with, where she seems almost to be walking out of the frame and into the room. She has her hands held out in front of her like a sleepwalker.[6] Sometimes, I find myself wanting to touch her, and I put my hands out so that they almost reach the hands in the painting.

1 **clutch** : hold tightly.
2 **hideous** [hɪdiəs] : frightful, repulsive, revolting.
3 **clay** : earth used for making bricks, pottery, ceramics, etc.
4 **slaved** : worked very hard.
5 **canvases** [kænvəsɪz] : paintings, also pieces of cloth used by artists for painting on.
6 **sleepwalker** : person walking while asleep.

Carlotta

Henri Matisse, 'L'Atelier sous le toit' (1903).

12 Read Part 4 and decide if the following statements are true or false.

	True	False
Edward kisses the image of Carlotta one night.		
Edward feels happy after the kiss.		
Edward believes that Carlotta has driven him mad.		
Edward feels bereft.		
Edward decides to tell his wife what he is going to do next.		

13 a How do you feel about the way in which Carlotta turns to the narrator?

  b Which of the two characters do you sympathise with? What influences you in your choice?

20 February

How am I going to write this? I pray that my darling Annie will never read it. But I have to say it. If I put it down on paper, it may not be so dangerous. If I don't say it, I feel the strength of my own feelings may cause me to explode. A strange thing happened last night. I had nearly finished another portrait of Carlotta: a close-up of her face taking up almost the entire canvas. I was painting the half-open mouth when suddenly I found that the brush had fallen out of my hand and my own lips were touching Carlotta's. I was kissing her image. This was bad enough. Worse, oh, so much worse, was what I was experiencing as my mouth came into contact with cold paint. I was as stirred [1] by this lifeless kiss as I had been the first time I had kissed the real Carlotta, all those years ago in the Art Room.

I tore myself away [2] from the painting, and went to lie on the studio sofa, feeling sick, and hot, as though some dreadful fever had seized hold [3] of me. I feel somewhat calmer now, writing this away from the studio, where she can't see me, but now that I am calmer, I can face the truth. She has enchanted me all over again. I want her. I wish we could be together once again. I think she has driven me mad.

Yesterday I found myself looking at her outstretched hands in the portrait I like best of all. The perspective has worked, I thought. She really does look as though she is about to walk out of the frame. I put my hands out and touched her painted ones. This must be what an electric shock feels like, I thought. I must stop. I must stop this madness now before it's too late. Oh, Carlotta, I am longing, hurting, burning for you! I cannot bear it.

10 April

The exhibition is over. It was an enormous success. Every single one of the portraits has been sold. The local paper called the show 'a moving tribute by one of her old schoolfriends to the tragic victim of a drowning accident'. I am a celebrity at school. Annie, I can see, is mightily relieved [4] to have the canvases out of the house. I am bereft. [5] I cannot live without her. I shall make her again. Differently this time. I shall take clay and fashion [6] her once more. I shall paint the clay in all the colours of her skin and hair ... bring her

1	**stirred** [stɜːd] : excited.	4	**relieved** : freed from anxiety or distress.
2	**tore myself away** : left, despite a strong desire to stay.	5	**bereft** : deprived, feeling great loss.
3	**seized hold** : taken possession.	6	**fashion** : make.

Carlotta

to some kind of life. I shall tell no one at all about this. It will be our secret. Carlotta's and mine.

1 May

It is done. Now we can be together. Carlotta, fetch me. Take me with you.   175

• •

Prediction

14 On the basis of what you have read in the diary entry dated 1 May, say what you think will happen next.

15 Before continuing, work with a partner and write your personal conclusion to the story.

Read the final part of the story and then answer the questions which follow.

• •

3 May 1993   Extract from the statement of Mrs Anne Stonely, submitted in evidence at the Coroner's Inquest

Beth was fast asleep in her room. We always had our supper, Edward and I, after she had gone to bed. I called him to come and eat, but he didn't come, so I went to find him. There was nothing strange about this. He often became   180
so absorbed in his work that he lost all track of time and place.

I went into the studio. I hadn't been in there for ages. I didn't know he had begun to work in clay. As soon as I saw him, slumped [1] like that against the model of a woman, I knew he was dead. His legs were trailing [2] on the floor. Her arms were around him. It was almost as if she were holding him   185
up. His head was thrown back. The woman's head had lolled [3] forward. It was horrible. They were tangled up [4] together. The worst thing of all was the hair. Her hair seemed to be filling his mouth. It almost looked as though he were eating it. I became hysterical. I knew who she was supposed to be. I

---

1 **slumped** : fallen heavily.

2 **trailing** : drawn along.

3 **lolled** : hung loosely.

4 **tangled up** : intertwined in a confused mass.

190 recognized the long black hair. It was Carlotta. I ran out of the studio screaming and my neighbour heard me, and phoned the police and our family doctor, Dr Cooper.

Later, Dr Cooper told me what he had found. I can't understand it. Edward, it seems, had choked[1] to death, even though they had no idea at all 195 of what might have choked him. There was no sign at all of anyone else having been in the studio, although the floor was awash[2] with water. No one knew where this had come from. Neither Dr Cooper nor the police could find any sign of a woman fashioned out of clay. They took me to the studio to show me, and I couldn't see her either. Not any more.

200 Dr Cooper says I must have become hysterical when I discovered Edward lying there dead, and imagined the whole thing. I must have. I hope that I did. Otherwise, what happened, and where Carlotta is now, are too horrible even to think about.

Detail from 'Umarmung'(Liebespaar II) 1917, by Egon Schiele.

1   **choked** [tʃəʊkt] : suffocated.   2   **awash** : covered.

16 a Who reports the final events?

b How does Annie realise that Edward is dead?

c How does Annie react at seeing Edward and Carlotta's statue "tangled up together"?

d What does Dr Cooper actually see in the studio?

Focus on Conclusion

17 Do you like the end of the story? Do you think it is:

☐ inconsistent   ☐ unexpected

☐ predictable   ☐ disappointing

☐ amazing   ☐ other

Tick appropriately, then justify your choice/s.

18 Is the actual outcome different from the one you wrote? If so, which do you prefer? Why?

Focus on Narration and Narrator

19 Tick appropriately:

a The story starts:

☐ in medias res

☐ through an introduction

b The story is narrated through:

☐ objective description of events

☐ dialogue

☐ subjective description of events with personal comments

c The story is told in diary form to:

☐ arouse expectation in the reader

☐ achieve a distancing effect

☐ create a sense of intimacy between the narrator and the reader

d The story is mainly told by a:

☐ first-person narrator who is involved in the story

☐ first-person narrator who is not involved in the story

e The main narrator's presence is perceived:

☐ only at the beginning of the story

☐ throughout the whole story

☐ at the end of the story

f The second narrator's presence serves:

☐ to clarify the position of the first narrator

☐ to reveal things about Carlotta

☐ to tell the readers about Edward's death

Discuss your answers in a group.

A Timeline to Summarise the Story

20 The story you have read is told in diary form and develops along a timeline. Write what you can remember next to the following headings to get a summary of the story. Refer to the diary-entries, if necessary!

19 November 1992 ....
....
....
....
....

22 November ....
....
....
....
....

29 November ....
....
....
....
....

10 February 1993 ....
....
....

Carlotta

....
....
20 February ....
....
....
....
....
10 April ....
....
....
....
....
1 May ....
....
....
....
....

21 What is the time span of the story?

22 The sections dated 3 May 1993 and 15 May 1993 have been omitted on purpose from the timeline. Can you say what their function in the story is?

Over to You

23 Think of different titles for the story, then discuss your choice/s with your classmates.

24 Say to what extent you think that Edward was responsible for Carlotta's death.

25 Have you ever experienced a difficult relationship? If your answer is yes, write a few lines to describe it; if your answer is no, write about a difficult relationship you have read about or seen in a film.

26 Write a letter to a friend suggesting that he/she reads *Carlotta*.

   a Briefly tell her/him about the plot.

   b Say why you like the story.

   c Explain how you analysed the story at school.

   d Add some personal comments.

Word-File

27 Revise all the new words you have met throughout the story you have just read: highlight the words which you think will be useful for communication and insert them in the following table.

Useful Words	Meaning

CROSS-CURRICULAR DATA

The Ghost Story

The Ghost story is mainly inspired by ancient legends and myths. It can be set in all sorts of places from an ordinary room to an old castle, either in the past or in the present.

The story is based on mystery and strange apparitions which have no rational explanation and cause a feeling of fear. The reader is totally involved in the narration and shares the feelings of the character that witnesses the apparition/s. The relationship between the living and the dead is at the core of the story.

The spirits of the dead manifest themselves in different ways. They may either be embodied in some form or disembodied. In that case they cause strange phenomena such as sounds and noises that come from nowhere, objects flying around by themselves, etc.

Moreover, the story may be centred on ghosts of dead people or on imaginary ones; that is, projections of people's fears under particular circumstances like the death of a beloved person, stress, psychological problems, etc.

Ghosts may be visible to some people but not to others or they might change their forms of appearance during a particular manifestation. Animals and things can be ghostly, too; there are, in fact, creatures and ghostly objects whose apparitions return after death: dogs, cats, owls, monkeys, ghost trains, coaches, ships, etc.

The apparitions of the dead haunt the living for various reasons: they cannot have peace until they have revealed a crime and punished the people responsible; they may have been buried in unhallowed ground and wish to be reburied where they can rest in peace; they may come back to seek vengeance, to protect someone, to predict future events, to make things unpleasant, etc.

Some famous authors of ghost stories are: Oscar Wilde, Henry James, Joseph Conrad, E.F. Benson, Marjorie Bowen, M.R. James, and M. Williams.

The Ghost Story

Note down:

1 the sources of inspiration of the ghost story.

2 whose feelings the reader shares.

3 how the spirits of the dead may come to life.

4 the kinds of ghosts that may be met.

5 the reasons why ghosts return to the world of the living.

UNIT TWO

Irrational Characters

"We all experience mirrors that distort"
Joyce Carol Oates

'Tain't So

by Maria Leach

Maria Leach

Main works:

The Beginning: Creation Myths around the World (1956)

The Rainbow Book of American Folk Tales and Legends (1958)

The Thing at the Foot of the Bed and Other Scary Tales (1959)

Noodles, Nitwits and Numskulls (1961)

How the People Sang the Mountains Up (1967)

Funk & Wagnalls Standard Dictionary of Folklore, Mythology and Legend (1972)

Whistle in the Graveyard: Folktales to Chill Your Bones, including the short story *"Tain't So'*, condensed by the author from a tale told by Emmy Seabrook in John Bennett's *'Doctor to the Dead'* published in 1947 (1974)

The Lion Sneezed: Folktales and Myths of the Cat (1977)

Riddle Me, Riddle Me, Ree (1977)

Don't Call Me Orphan (1979)

The Luck Book (1979)

The Importance of Being a Wit: The Insults of Oscar Wilde (1997)

The Ultimate Insult (1997)

'Tain't So

BEFORE READING

A Brief Trip into the World of the Dead

1 Work with a partner and match the nouns on the left with their definitions on the right, by using arrows. One has already been done for you!

CORPSE   a long narrow wooden box in which a
                                corpse is buried or cremated

GRAVEYARD   a funeral

GRAVE   stone on top of or at the head of a grave
                                with the name, etc. of the person buried there

GRAVESTONE   cemetery

GRAVE-DIGGER   a dead body

HEARSE   a trench dug in the ground to receive a coffin
                                on burial

COFFIN   a person who digs graves

BURIAL   a vehicle for conveying the coffin at a funeral

Check your answers in your monolingual dictionary.

2 Look at the title of the story:

'Tain't So

Ain't is a non-standard form of English and is short for:

a am not

b is not

c are not

d has not

e have not

Is a, b, c, d or e the right match for the title? What helps you to decide?

Compare your answers with your classmates and then suggest what the story is about.

3 Here are the first lines of the story. They are given in scrambled order. Number them to reconstruct the beginning of the story, then listen to the cassette to check.

☐ 'You are dying,' said the doctor.

☐ So they put the old man in his coffin; they carried him to church and had his funeral; then they carried him to the graveyard and buried him.

☐ ''Tain't so!' said old man Dinkins. But the next day he was dead.

☐ Old Mr Dinkins was very ill, so they sent for the doctor. When the doctor came, old man Dinkins said, 'There's nothing the matter with me!'

4 Who does the pronoun 'they' refer to?

5 Complete the following table.

What was the matter with old Mr Dinkins?	
What did the doctor say?	
How did old Mr Dinkins react to what the doctor said?	
What happened the next day?	

Compare your answers with your classmates.

6 What do the expressions 'There's nothing the matter with me!' and ''Tain't so!' tell you about the sort of person Mr Dinkins is.

• •

Old Mr Dinkins was very ill, so they sent for the doctor. When the doctor came, old man Dinkins said, 'There's nothing the matter with me!'

'You are dying, 'said the doctor.

''Tain't so!' said old man Dinkins. But the next day he was dead. So they
5   put the old man in his coffin; they carried him to church and had his funeral;
then they carried him to the graveyard and buried him.

7 Listen to Part 2 and fill in the following table:

		1st Neighbour	2nd Neighbour	A Townsman
Setting:	time			
	place			
What he saw/heard				
What he did afterwards				

The next morning a neighbour passing the graveyard on his way to work saw old man Dinkins sitting on the graveyard fence.

'Hello, there! I thought you were dead,' said the neighbour.

''Tain't so!' said old man Dinkins. 10

The neighbour went and told old Mrs Dinkins that her husband was sitting on the graveyard fence and said he was *not* dead.

'Pay no attention,' said the widow. 'He's foolish.'

Later on another neighbour passing by the graveyard heard someone say, 'Hello, Tom!' 15

71

'Hello,' said Tom and stopped for a chat. 'It's you, is it?'

'Sure,' said old man Dinkins.

'I heard you were dead.'

''Tain't so!'

20 'I heard about the burial.'

'Well, you can see I'm not buried.'

'That's so,' said the neighbour and went on his way, somewhat puzzled.

The next day one of the townsmen was passing by the graveyard on horseback. He heard someone say, 'Hello,' and stopped to see who it was. He 25 saw a very old gentleman sitting on the fence, who said, 'What's the news from town?'

'Not much news, except old man Dinkins is dead.'

''Tain't so!'

'That's what they said.'

30 'Well, 'tain't so.'

'How do you know?' said the man.

'I'm Dinkins.'

'Oh!' said the man and rode away from the place pretty fast.

He stopped at the next store and said, 'There's a funny old fellow sitting 35 on the graveyard fence who says he is old man Dinkins.'

'Can't possibly be,' said the storekeeper.

'Why not?'

'Because old man Dinkins is dead.'

8 How many days elapsed from Mr Dinkins' funeral to the moment when he said 'I'm Dinkins'?

9 What was the widow's opinion about her dead husband?

10 a How did all the people passing by the graveyard feel in front of Mr Dinkins' ghost?

b How did the ghost feel while facing the people passing by?

You may choose one or more expressions from the list in the box below:

scared to death	at ease	excited	upset	puzzled	angry
indifferent	resigned	horrified	nervous	relaxed	disturbed

11 The author uses the same verb to indicate what the first neighbour, the second neighbour and the townsman were doing. What is it?

Who Said What?

12 Read the following jumbled quotations from parts 1 and 2 and write the names of the characters that said them on the lines provided below.

a .... 'Can't possibly be.'

b .... 'There's nothing the matter with me!'

c .... 'Not much news, except old man Dinkins is dead.'

d .... 'Hello, there! I thought you were dead.'

e .... 'He's foolish.'

f .... 'I heard about the burial.'

Check your answers by reading the text.

13 a What is the matter with dead Mr Dinkins?

    b Why do you think Mr Dinkins behaves as he does?

    c How you think the story will develop.

14 Listen to the final part of the story and fill in the following Character-Chart on Mr Dinkins.

Full name	
Age	
Reputation	
Where he lived	
When he died	

Read the text to check your answers.

This kept going on week after week, month after month. The whole town
40 knew that old man Dinkins was dead; but old man Dinkins sat on the
graveyard fence saying, ''Tain't so.'

After much talk and consultation the townspeople decided to hold *another*
burial service.

So they said the burial service over the old man's grave for a second time
45 and set up his gravestone.

The words on the gravestone said:

The next day when old man Dinkins crawled [1] out of his grave, he read
55 what the stone said. He read it over two or three times.

'Well – maybe so,' he said. He hasn't yelled [2] at anybody from the
graveyard fence since then.

---

1 **crawled** : moved slowly.   2 **yelled** : shouted or made a loud noise.

Focus on Actions

15 Try to justify the following actions:

    a The townspeople decided to hold another burial service.

    b Mr Dinkins' ghost read what the stone said two or three times.

    c Mr Dinkins' ghost said 'Well – maybe so'.

Focus on Conclusion

A story may be open- or closed-ended.

16 In an open-ended story there may be further developments.

In a closed-ended story the events narrated come to a natural or logical conclusion.

    a Is the story you have read open- or closed-ended?

    b Why do you think the writer has decided to conclude the story in this way?

Over to You

17 Did the story appeal to you? Why/why not?

18 What shocked or surprised you particularly?

19 Do you think that Mr Dinkins' ghost is an irrational one? Why/why not?

20 Imagine dramatising this story to make a film: would it be difficult? Which changes from the narrative version would you make?

Word-File

21 Revise all the new words you have met throughout the story you have just read: highlight the words which you think will be useful for communication and insert them in the following table.

Useful Words	Meaning

The Man Who Loved Flowers

by Stephen King

Stephen King

Stephen King was born in September 1946, in Portland, Maine. His family moved to Fort Wayne, Indiana in 1949. Shortly after, his father left the family and they never heard from him again. King's family moved to Durham, Maine in 1958. King discovered a box of science-fiction and horror books at an aunt's house, which marked the beginning of his fascination with horror.

King attended Lisbon Falls High School, and then went to the University of Maine at Orono, from which he graduated in 1970 with a BS in English and a Minor in Speech.

He married Tabitha Spruce, whom he met at university, and taught English at Hampden Academy, living in a trailer and writing for magazines as an extra source of income. He later became a full-time writer.

In 1980 King moved to Bangor, Maine, where he still lives with his wife and three children. He often writes under the pseudonym of Richard Bachman: *Rage* (1977); *The Long Walk* (1979); *Roadwork* (1981); *The Running Man* (1982); *Thinner* (1984).

Main works:

Carrie (1974)

'Salem's Lot (1975)

The Shining (1977)

Night Shift (from which the story you are going to read is taken) (1978)

Christine (1983)

It (1986)

Misery (1987)

The Tommyknockers (1987)

The Dark Half (1989)

Four Past Midnight (1990)

Insomnia (1994)

Desperation (1996)

The Man Who Loved Flowers

BEFORE READING

1 Look at the following picture and the title of the story and say what you expect to read about.

The Man
Who Loved Flowers

2 Listen to the beginning of the story and complete the following table.

Setting:	Time	
	Place	
Characters involved		
What the old lady is doing		
What the old lady says		
What the old lady thinks		

Compare your answers with your partner, then read the text to check them.

• •

On an early evening in May of 1963, a young man with his hand in his pocket walked briskly up New York's Third Avenue. The air was soft and beautiful, the sky was darkening by slow degrees from blue to the calm and lovely violet of dusk. There are people who love the city, and this was one of the nights that made them love it. Everyone standing in the doorways of the ⁵ delicatessens and dry-cleaning shops and restaurants seemed to be smiling. An old lady pushing two bags of groceries in an old baby pram grinned [1] at

---

1   **grinned** : smiled.

79

the young man and hailed [1] him: 'Hey, beautiful!' The young man gave her a half-smile and raised his hand in a wave.

10 *She passed on her way, thinking: He's in love.*

• •

Focus on the setting and say:

3 **a** which details are given relevance.

  b whether you get a positive or negative impression and why.

  c through whose eyes the setting is seen.

Andy Warhol, 'Flowers' (1964).

Read Part 2 and do the activities which follow.

• •

He had that look about him. He was dressed in a light grey suit, the narrow tie pulled down a little, his top collar button undone. His hair was dark and cut short. His complexion was fair, his eyes a light blue. Not an extraordinary face, but on this soft spring evening, on this avenue, in May of 15 1963, he *was* beautiful, and the old woman found herself thinking with a moment's sweet nostalgia that in spring anyone can be beautiful ... if they're hurrying to meet the one of their dreams for dinner and maybe dancing after.

---

1 **hailed** : greeted.

The Man Who Loved Flowers

Spring is the only season when nostalgia never seems to turn bitter, and she went on her way glad that she had spoken to him and glad he had returned the compliment by raising his hand in half-salute. 20

The young man crossed Sixty-third Street, walking with a bounce [1] in his step and that same half-smile on his lips. Part way up the block, an old man stood beside a chipped [2] green handcart filled with flowers – the predominant colour was yellow; a yellow fever of jonquils and late crocuses. The old man also had carnations and a few hothouse tea roses, mostly yellow [25] and white. He was eating a pretzel [3] and listening to a bulky transistor radio that was sitting kitty-corner [4] on his handcart.

The radio poured out bad news that no one listened to: a hammer murderer was still on the loose; [5] JFK had declared that the situation in a little Asian country called Vietnam ('Vite-num' the guy reading the news called it) [30] would bear watching; [6] an unidentified woman had been pulled from the East River; a grand jury had failed to indict [7] a crime overlord in the current city administration's war on heroin; the Russians had exploded a nuclear device. None of it seemed real, none of it seemed to matter. The air was soft and sweet. Two men with beer bellies stood outside a bakery, pitching [8] [35] nickels and ribbing [9] each other. Spring trembled on the edge of summer, and in the city, summer is the season of dreams.

The young man passed the flower stand and the sound of the bad news faded. He hesitated, looked over his shoulder, and thought it over. He reached into his coat pocket and touched the something in there again. For a [40] moment his face seemed puzzled, lonely, almost haunted, and then, as his hand left the pocket, it regained its former expression of eager expectation.

He turned back to the flower stand, smiling. He would bring her some flowers, that would please her. He loved to see her eyes light up with surprise and joy when he brought her a surprise – little things, because he [45] was far from rich. A box of candy. [10] A bracelet. Once only a bag of Valencia oranges, because he knew they were Norma's favourite.

1	**a bounce** : energy, vitality.	6	**bear watching** : be of interest to follow.
2	**chipped** : broken or cut on the surface.	7	**indict** [ɪndaɪt] : officially accuse.
3	**pretzel** : crispy salted biscuit in the shape of a knot or a stick.	8	**pitching** : throwing, tossing.
4	**kitty-corner** : diagonally.	9	**ribbing** : making fun of.
5	**on the loose** : free to move around and harm people.	10	**candy** : sweets.

Use your own words and...

4 a Write a description of the young man.

  b Re-write the bad news broadcast on the radio.

    • ....

    • ....

    • ....

    • ....

    • ....

  c Study the following examples:

He thought he was in love	INDIRECT THOUGHT
He thought: "I'm in love"	DIRECT THOUGHT
He was in love	FREE INDIRECT THOUGHT
I'm in love	FREE DIRECT THOUGHT

    Now look back at lines 43-47 and say if the type of thought presented is:

    ☐ direct   ☐ indirect

    ☐ free direct   ☐ free indirect

5 Read Part 3 and write the words in the box on the 'correct line, by referring to the context in which they are used.

seam	spill	pitching	stems	tooting	ducked	knitted
pouches	jittered	gutter	grinned	sour	zoomed	stock

adjectives : ....

....

nouns : ....

....

verbs : ....

....

6 Try to guess the meaning of the words from the context.

Word	Line	Your Guess	Dictionary Meaning
stock			
knitted			
pouches			
jittered			
zoomed			
sour			
grinned			
gutter			
ducked			
tooting			
pitching			
stems			
spill			
seam			

Check in your monolingual dictionary.

• •

'My young friend,' the flower vendor said, as the man in the grey suit came back, running his eyes over the stock in the handcart. The vendor was maybe sixty-eight, wearing a torn grey knitted sweater and a soft cap in spite 50
of the warmth of the evening. His face was a map of wrinkles, his eyes were deep in pouches, and a cigarette jittered between his fingers. But he also remembered how it was to be young in the spring – young and so much in love that you practically zoomed everywhere. The vendor's face was normally sour, but now he smiled a little, just as the old woman pushing the 55
groceries had, because this guy was such an obvious case. He brushed

pretzel crumbs from the front of his baggy [1] sweater and thought: If this kid were sick, they'd have him in intensive care right now.

'How much are your flowers?' the young man asked.

60 'I'll make you up a nice bouquet for a dollar. Those tea roses, they're hothouse. Cost a little more, seventy cents apiece. I sell you half a dozen for three dollars and fifty cents.'

'Expensive,' the young man said.

'Nothing good comes cheap, my young friend. Didn't your mother ever 65 teach you that?'

The young man grinned. 'She might have mentioned it at that.'

'Sure. Sure she did. I give you half a dozen, two red, two yellow, two white. Can't do no better than that, can I? Put in some baby's breath – they love that – and fill it out with some fern. Nice. Or you can have the bouquet 70 for a dollar.'

'They?' the young man asked, still smiling.

'My young friend,' the flower vendor said, flicking his cigarette butt into the gutter and returning the smile, 'no one buys flowers for themselves in May. It's like a national law, you understand what I mean?'

75 The young man thought of Norma, her happy, surprised eyes and her gentle smile, and he ducked his head a little. 'I guess I do at that,' he said.

'Sure you do. What do you say?'

'Well, what do *you* think?'

'I'm gonna tell you what I think. Hey! Advice is still free, isn't it?'

80 The young man smiled and said, 'I guess it's the only thing left that is.'

'You're damn tooting it is,' the flower vendor said. 'Okay, my young friend. If the flowers are for your mother, you get her the bouquet. A few jonquils, a few crocuses, some lily of the valley. She don't spoil it by saying, "Oh Junior I love them how much did they cost oh that's too much don't you 85 know enough not to throw your money around?"'

The young man threw his head back and laughed.

The Vendor said, 'But if it's your girl, that's a different thing, my son, and you know it. You bring her the tea roses and she don't turn into an accountant, you take my meaning? Hey! she's gonna throw her arms around 90 your neck –'

'I'll take the tea roses,' the young man said, and this time it was the flower vendor's turn to laugh. The two men pitching nickels glanced over, smiling.

1 **baggy** : big, loose.

'Hey, kid!' one of them called. 'You wanna buy a weddin' ring cheap? I'll sell you mine ... I don't want it no more.'

The young man grinned and blushed to the roots of his dark hair. 95

The flower vendor picked out six tea roses, snipped the stems a little, spritzed them with water, and wrapped them in a large conical spill.

'Tonight's weather looks just the way you'd want it,' the radio said. 'Fair and mild, temps in the mid to upper sixties, perfect for a little rooftop stargazing, if you're the romantic type. Enjoy, Greater New York, enjoy!' 100

The flower vendor Scotch-taped the seam of the paper spill and advised the young man to tell his lady that a little sugar added to the water she put them in would preserve them longer.

'I'll tell her,' the young man said. He held out a five-dollar bill. 'Thank you.' 105

'Just doing the job, my young friend,' the vendor said, giving him a dollar and two quarters. His smile grew a bit sad. 'Give her a kiss for me.'

7 Use the words in the box below to complete Part 4, then listen to the cassette to check your answers.

| right | ninth | blast | cop | roses | quarter |
| vague | alert | mirror | wagon | softly |

On the radio, the Four Seasons began singing 'Sherry'. The young man pocketed his change and went on up the street, eyes wide and .... and eager, looking not so much around him at the life ebbing and flowing up and down 110 Third Avenue as inward and ahead, anticipating. But certain things did impinge[1]: a mother pulling a baby in a .... , the baby's face comically smeared with ice cream; a little girl jumping rope and singsonging out her rhyme: 'Betty and Henry up in a tree, K-I-S-S-I-N-G! First comes love, then comes marriage, here comes Henry with a baby carriage!' Two women stood outside a 115 washateria, smoking and comparing pregnancies. A group of men were looking in a hardware-store window at a gigantic colour TV with a four-figure price tag –

1 **impinge** : make an impression.

85

a baseball game was on, and all the players' faces looked green. The playing field
was a .... strawberry colour, and the New York Mets were leading the
Phillies by a score of six to one in the top of the ....

120

He walked on, carrying the flowers, unaware that the two women outside the
washateria had stopped talking for a moment and had watched him wistfully as
he walked by with his paper of tea .... ; their days of receiving flowers
were long over. He was unaware of a young traffic .... who stopped the
cars at the intersection of Third and Sixty-ninth with a .... on his whistle
to let him cross; the cop was engaged himself and recognized the dreamy
expression on the young man's face from his own shaving ...., where he
had often seen it lately. He was unaware of the two teen-aged girls who passed
him going the other way and then clutched themselves [1] and giggled. [2]

125

At Seventy-third Street he stopped and turned .... This street was a
little darker, lined with brownstones and walk-down restaurants with Italian
names. Three blocks down, a stickball [3] game was going on in the fading light.

130

The young man did not go that far; half a block down he turned into a narrow lane.

Now the stars were out, gleaming [4] .... , and the lane was dark and
shadowy, lined with the vague shape of garbage [5] cans. The young man was alone
now – no, not quite. A wavering yowl [6] rose in the purple gloom, and the young
man frowned. [7] It was some tomcat's love song, and there was nothing pretty
about *that*.

135

He walked more slowly, and glanced at his watch. It was .... of eight and
Norma should be just –

140

• •

8 Read through Part 5 and say what you think will happen.

1	**clutched themselves** : held each other tightly.	5	**garbage** : rubbish.
2	**giggled** : laughed in a silly manner.	6	**wavering yowl** : unsteady loud cry.
3	**stickball** : American street game, similar to baseball.	7	**frowned** : brought his eyebrows together and wrinkled the skin on his forehead to express worry.
4	**gleaming** : shining faintly.		

The Man Who Loved Flowers

Then he saw her, coming towards him from the courtyard, wearing dark blue slacks [1] and a sailor blouse that made his heart ache. It was always a surprise seeing her for the first time, it was always a sweet shock – she looked so *young*.

Now his smile shone out – *radiated* out, and he walked faster. 145

'Norma!' he said.

She looked up and smiled ... but as they drew together, the smile faded.

His own smile trembled a little, and he felt a moment's disquiet. Her face over the sailor blouse suddenly seemed blurred. [2] It was getting darker now ... could he have been mistaken? Surely not. It *was* Norma. 150

'I brought you flowers,' he said in a happy relief, and handed the paper spill to her.

She looked at them for a moment, smiled – and handed them back.

'Thank you, but you're mistaken,' she said. 'My name is –'

• •

9 Read to the end of the story and say who/what the highlighted words refer to:

• •

'Norma,' he whispered, and pulled the short-handled hammer out of his 155 coat pocket where it had been all along. ' They 're for you, Norma ... it was always for you ... all for you.'

She backed away, her face a round white blur, her mouth an opening black O of terror, and she wasn't Norma, Norma was dead, she had been dead for ten years, and it didn't matter because she was going to scream and 160 he swung [3] the hammer to stop the scream, to kill the scream, and as he swung the hammer the spill of flowers fell out of his hand, the spill spilled and broke open, spilling red, white, and yellow tea roses beside the dented [4] trash cans where the cats made alien love in the dark, screaming in love, screaming, screaming. 165

He swung the hammer and she didn't scream, but she might scream because she wasn't Norma, none of them were Norma, and he swung the hammer, swung the hammer, swung the hammer. She wasn't Norma and so he swung the hammer, as he had done five other times.

1	**slacks** : casual trousers.	3	**swung** : moved to and fro.
2	**blurred** : unclear, out of focus.	4	**dented** : hollowed in by pressure or a heavy stroke.

170   Some unknown time later he slipped the hammer back into his inner coat pocket and backed away from the dark shadow sprawled [1] on the cobblestones, [2] away from the litter of tea roses by the garbage cans. He turned and left the narrow lane. It was full dark now. The stickball players had gone in. If there were bloodstains on his suit, they wouldn't show, not

175   in the dark, not in the soft late spring dark, and *her* name had not been Norma but he knew what his name was. It was ... was ...

Love.

His name was love, and he walked these dark streets because Norma was waiting for him . And he would find her. Some day soon.

180   He began to smile. A bounce came into his step as he walked on down Seventy-third Street. A middle-aged married couple sitting on the steps of their building watched him go by, head cocked, [3] eyes afar away, a half-smile on his lips. When he had passed by the woman said, 'How come *you* never look that way any more?'

185   'Huh?'

'Nothing,' she said, but she watched the young man in the grey suit disappear into the gloom of the encroaching [4] night and thought that if there was anything more beautiful than springtime, it was young love.

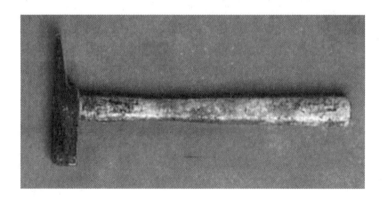

1 **sprawled** : spread out.

2 **cobblestones** : rounded stones used for covering the surface of roads.

3 **cocked** : turned slightly to one side.

4 **encroaching** : advancing gradually.

The Man Who Loved Flowers

10 Complete the following table.

The girl's reaction at seeing the hammer	
How long Norma had been dead	
Number of girls previously killed by the hammer murderer	
Why the bloodstains on the young man's suit did not show	

Focus on Narration

11 In the story you have just read there is a detail, which on first reading appears irrelevant, hinting at the murderer who will be seen 'in action' only towards the end of the story. Can you find the 'detail'?

12 Why do you think the narrator has used such a device (anticipation)? Tick appropriately, then discuss your answers with your classmates.

- [ ] to produce expectation in the reader.
- [ ] to let the reader think and reconstruct the story after its actual ending.
- [ ] to identify the murderer without letting the reader realise it.

The Plot of the Story

13 Here are the main points of the story you have just read in jumbled order. Number them to reconstruct the plot of the story.

- [ ] The young man stopped at a flower stand and had a conversation with the flower vendor.
- [ ] An old lady greeted the young man and thought he was in love.
- [ ] One evening in May 1963 a young man walked along New York's Third Avenue.
- [ ] The radio news said that a hammer murderer was still on the loose.
- [ ] The young man gave the girl the flowers.

☐ The young man bought a bunch of tea roses.

☐ The young man saw a girl approaching and called her.

☐ The young man pulled a hammer out of his jacket and killed the girl.

☐ Seventy-third street was darker than the other streets.

☐ The young man turned into Seventy-third street.

14 Can you identify the climax or point of greatest tension in the story?

A Summary of the Story

15 Read the following summary of the story and say what is missing:

One evening a young man walked in New York's Third Avenue. He stopped at a flower vendor's and bought a bunch of flowers. He saw a girl approaching and gave her the flowers. Then he killed her with a hammer.

16 Work with a partner and discuss why such a summary would tell someone new to the story very little. Then try to improve it.

Focus on Language

17 Look back at Part 3 and observe the way in which the flower vendor speaks: he uses a few ungrammatical forms. List them in the table below, then underline and correct the mistakes. Something has already been written for you!

Ungrammatical Forms	Line	Correct Forms
Cost a little more than 70 cents apiece	61	They cost a little more than 70 cents apiece.
	68	
	68	
	83	
	88	
	88	
	106	

The Man Who Loved Flowers

American Expressions

18 Throughout the story there are a few expressions in American English. Work with a partner, look for the American expressions and write their British equivalents in the table below.

American Expression	Line	British Equivalent
	79	
		You're quite right
	89	
	93	

Picturing the Story

19 Imagine that a film has been made from the story and that you have been asked to choose four 'still pictures' from the film to advertise it. What pictures would you choose? First work on your own, then compare your choices with your classmates.

Word-File

20 Revise all the new words you have met throughout the story you have just read: highlight the words which you think will be useful for communication and insert them in the following table.

Useful Words	Meaning

Mr Loveday's Little Outing

by Evelyn Waugh

Evelyn Waugh

Evelyn Waugh was born in October 1903 in London, into a middle-class family.

He attended Lancing School and won a scholarship to Oxford. He became an agnostic and a revolutionary and learnt to drink and dress according to the aesthetic principles.

In 1924 he returned home without having completed his education and having run into debt. He worked as a teacher in North Wales. In 1928 he married Evelyn Gardner and became a Roman Catholic. He divorced in 1930. Throughout the 1930's he travelled in Europe, and went to the East, Africa and South America.

Waugh remarried in 1937 settling in the West Country. During World War II he served in the Royal Marines.

He died in April 1966.

Main works:

Decline and Fall (1928)

Black Mischief (1932)

A Handful of Dust (1934)

Mr Loveday's Little Outing and Other Sad Stories (1936)

Brideshead Revisited (1945)

Sword of Honour (1965)

Mr Loveday's Little Outing

BEFORE READING

1 How do you judge people? Which of the following aspects contributes to determining your opinion of a person? Put a cross ✗ in the appropriate column:

	not at all	a little	quite a lot	very much
personality				
behaviour				
way of speaking				
physical appearance				
social class				
religious beliefs				
tastes, interests, habits				
attitude to other people and to life				

Compare your answers with your classmates.

2 What do you associate the concept of insanity with?
Complete the following spidergram.

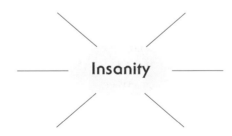

Insanity

Evelyn Waugh

3 Read the beginning of the story and complete the following chart.

Who the characters speaking are	
Where Angela's father is	
Who suggests to Angela that she should visit her father	
How long Lord Moping has been in the Asylum	
What the weather was like on the day of Lady Moping's party	
What happened at six o'clock	
How often Lady Moping visits her husband	

• •

'You will not find your father greatly changed,' remarked Lady Moping, as the car turned into the gates of the County Asylum. [1]

'Will he be wearing a uniform?' asked Angela.

'No, dear, of course not. He is receiving the very best attention.'

5   It was Angela's first visit and it was being made at her own suggestion.

Ten years had passed since the showery day in late summer when Lord Moping had been taken away; a day of confused but bitter memories for her; the day of Lady Moping's annual garden party, always bitter, confused that day by the caprice of the weather which, remaining clear and brilliant with promise

10   until the arrival of the first guests, had suddenly blackened into a squall. [2]

There had been a scuttle [3] for cover; the marquee [4] had capsized; [5] frantic carrying of cushions and chairs; a table-cloth lofted to the boughs of the

1   **Asylum** : mental or psychiatric hospital.

2   **squall** : storm with violent wind, rain or snow.

3   **scuttle** : run.

4   **marquee** [maːkiː] : tent used for open-air events like parties.

5   **capsized** : fallen on its side.

monkey-puzzler, [1] fluttering [2] in the rain; a bright period and the cautious emergence of guests on to the soggy [3] lawns; another squall; another twenty minutes of sunshine. It had been an abominable afternoon, culminating at about six o'clock in her father's attempted suicide.

Lord Moping habitually threatened suicide on the occasion of the garden party; that year he had been found black in the face, hanging by his braces [4] in the orangery; some neighbours, who were sheltering there from the rain, set him on his feet again, and before dinner a van had called for him. Since then Lady Moping had paid seasonal calls at the asylum and returned in time for tea, rather reticent of her experience.

Many of her neighbours were inclined to be critical of Lord Moping's accommodation. He was not, of course, an ordinary inmate. [5] He lived in a separate wing of the asylum, specially devoted to the segregation of wealthier lunatics. These were given every consideration which their foibles [6] permitted. They might choose their own clothes (Many indulged in the liveliest fancies), smoke the most expensive brands of cigars and, on the

15

20

25

---

1 **monkey-puzzler** : pinetree.

2 **fluttering** : flying, moving rapidly.

3 **soggy** : very wet.

4 **braces** : straps to hold up or support the trousers.

5 **inmate** : a person who is kept in a mental hospital, prison, etc.

6 **foibles** [fɔɪblz] : foolish, harmless habits.

anniversaries of their certification, entertain any other inmates for whom
30 they had an attachment to private dinner parties.

The fact remained, however, that it was far from being the most expensive
kind of institution; the uncompromising address, 'COUNTY HOME FOR
MENTAL DEFECTIVES', stamped across the notepaper, worked on the
uniforms of their attendants, painted, even, upon a prominent hoarding [1] at
35 the main entrance, suggested the lowest associations. From time to time, with
less or more tact, her friends attempted to bring to Lady Moping's notice
particulars of seaside nursing homes, of 'qualified practitioners with large
private grounds suitable for the charge of nervous or difficult cases,' but she
accepted them lightly; when her son came of age he might make any changes
40 that he thought fit; meanwhile she felt no inclination to relax her economical
regime; her husband had betrayed her basely on the one day in the year
when she looked for loyal support, and was far better off than he deserved.

• •

4 Say if the Story Starts :

a ☐ through an introduction

b ☐ in medias res (directly in the middle of a situation)

Advantages

5 What are the four advantages that richer lunatics had in the Asylum? One has already been written for you.

a They lived in a separate section of the Asylum.

b ....
....

c ....
....

d ....
....

1   **hoarding** : big board on which notices and adverts are put.

Mr Loveday's Little Outing

6 Go on reading and answer the following questions.

a What was strange about the chair near the radiator?

b What was Lord Moping's talk centred on?

c What does the expression 'You don't mean he's cuckoo, too?' mean?

• •

A few lonely figures in great-coats were shuffling[1] and loping[2] about the
park.

'Those are the lower-class lunatics,' observed Lady Moping. 'There is a   45
very nice little flower garden for people like your father. I sent them some
cuttings last year.'

They drove past the blank, yellow brick facade to the doctor's private
entrance and were received by him in the 'visitors room', set aside for
interviews of this kind. The window was protected on the inside by bars and   50
wire netting; there was no fireplace; when Angela nervously attempted to move
her chair further from the radiator, she found that it was screwed[3] to the floor.

'Lord Moping is quite ready to see you,' said the doctor.

'How is he?'

'Oh, very well, very well indeed, I'm glad to say. He had rather a nasty   55
cold some time ago, but apart from that his condition is excellent. He spends
a lot of his time in writing.'

They heard a shuffling, skipping[4] sound approaching along the flagged[5]
passage. Outside the door a high peevish[6] voice, which Angela recognized as
her father's, said: 'I haven't the time, I tell you. Let them come back later.'   60

A gentler tone, with a slight rural burr,[7] replied, 'Now come along. It is a
purely formal audience. You need stay no longer than you like.'

Then the door was pushed open (it had no lock or fastening) and Lord
Moping came into the room. He was attended by an elderly little man with
full white hair and an expression of great kindness.   65

'That is Mr Loveday who acts as Lord Moping's attendant.'

1	**shuffling** : walking with difficulty.	5	**flagged** : covered with square or rectangular stones.
2	**loping** : walking very quickly, almost jumping.	6	**peevish** : bad-tempered, easily irritated.
3	**screwed** : fastened, attached.		
4	**skipping** : light jumping.	7	**a slight rural burr** : refers to a prolonged pronunciation of the letter "r".

99

'Secretary,' said Lord Moping. He moved with a jogging gait [1] and shook hands with his wife.

'This is Angela. You remember Angela, don't you?'

70 'No, I can't say that I do. What does she want?'

'We just came to see you.'

'Well, you have come at an exceedingly inconvenient time. I am very busy. Have you typed out that letter to the Pope yet, Loveday?'

'No, my lord. If you remember, you asked me to look up the figures about

75 the Newfoundland fisheries first?'

'So I did. Well, it is fortunate, as I think the whole letter will have to be redrafted. A great deal of new information has come to light since luncheon. A great deal ... You see, my dear, I am fully occupied.' He turned his restless, quizzical [2] eyes upon Angela. 'I suppose you have come about the Danube.

80 Well, you must come again later. Tell them it will be all right, quite all right, but I have not had time to give my full attention to it. Tell them that.'

'Very well, Papa.'

'Anyway,' said Lord Moping rather petulantly, 'it is a matter of secondary importance. There is the Elbe and the Amazon and the Tigris to be dealt with

85 first, eh, Loveday? ... *Danube* indeed. Nasty little river. I'd only call it a stream myself. Well, can't stop, nice of you to come. I would do more for you if I could, but you see how I'm fixed. Write to me about it. That's it. *Put it in black and white.*'

And with that he left the room.

90 'You see,' said the doctor, 'he is in excellent condition. He is putting on weight, eating and sleeping excellently. In fact, the whole tone of his system is above reproach.' [3]

The door opened again and Loveday returned.

'Forgive my coming back, sir, but I was afraid that the young lady might

95 be upset at his lordship's not knowing her. You mustn't mind him, miss. Next time he'll be very pleased to see you. It's only today he's put out [4] on account of being behindhand with his work. You see, sir, all this week I've been helping in the library and I haven't been able to get all his lordship's reports typed out. And he's got muddled [5] with his card index. That's all it is.

100 He doesn't mean any harm.'

---

1 **gait** : a particular way of walking.

2 **quizzical** : seeming to ask a question without speaking.

3 **above reproach** : in good health.

4 **put out** : annoyed, upset.

5 **he's got muddled** : he's got confused.

Mr Loveday's Little Outing

'What a nice man,' said Angela, when Loveday had gone back to his charge.

'Yes. I don't know what we should do without old Loveday. Everybody loves him, staff and patients alike.'

'I remember him well. It's a great comfort to know that you are able to get 105 such good warders,'[1] said Lady Moping; 'people who don't know, say such foolish things about asylums.'

'Oh, but Loveday isn't a warder,' said the doctor.

'You don't mean he's cuckoo, too?' said Angela.

The doctor corrected her. 'He is an *inmate*. It is rather an interesting case. 110 He has been here for thirty-five years.'

'But I've never seen anyone saner,' said Angela.

'He certainly has that air,' said the doctor, 'and in the last twenty years we have treated him as such. He is the life and soul of the place. Of course he is not one of the private patients, but we allow him to mix freely with them. He 115 plays billiards excellently, does conjuring tricks[2] at the concert, mends their gramophones, valets them,[3] helps them in their crossword puzzles and various – er – hobbies. We allow them to give him small tips for services rendered, and he must by now have amassed quite a little fortune. He has a way with even the most troublesome of them. An invaluable man about the 120 place.'

'Yes, but why is he here?'

• •

7 What first impression do you get of Mr Loveday? Can you guess why he is one of the Asylum's inmates?

Continue reading and see if you were right.

---

1   **warders** : male attendants.

2   **conjuring tricks** : when something is made to appear or disappear as if by magic.

3   **valets** [vælеɪz] **them** : acts as their personal attendant.

101

'Well, it is rather sad. When he was a very young man he killed somebody –
a young woman quite unknown to him, whom he knocked off her bicycle
125 and then throttled.[1] He gave himself up immediately afterwards and has
been here ever since.'

'But surely he is perfectly safe now. Why is he not let out?'

'Well, I suppose if it was to anyone's interest, he would be. He has no
relatives except a step-sister who lives in Plymouth. She used to visit him at
130 one time, but she hasn't been for years now. He's perfectly happy here and I
can assure you *we* aren't going to take the first steps in turning him out. He's
far too useful to us.'

'But it doesn't seem fair,' said Angela.

'Look at your father,' said the doctor. 'He'd be quite lost without Loveday
135 to act as his secretary.'

'It doesn't seem fair.'

• •

Focus on Mr Loveday and say something about:

8 a his physical appearance.

   b his role in the asylum.

   c his youth.

9 List the 3 reasons why Mr Loveday is not let out of the Asylum:

   a ....

      ....

   b ....

      ....

   c ....

      ....

Continue reading, then do the activity which follows.

1   **throttled** [θrɒtld] : strangled.

Angela left the asylum, oppressed by a sense of injustice. Her mother was unsympathetic. [1]

'Think of being locked up in a looney bin [2] all one's life.'

'He attempted to hang himself in the orangery,' replied Lady Moping, *'in front of the Chester-Martins.'* [140]

'I don't mean Papa. I mean Mr Loveday.'

'I don't think I know him.'

'Yes, the looney they have put to look after Papa.'

'Your father's secretary. A very decent sort of man, I thought, and [145] eminently suited to his work.'

Angela left the question for the time, but returned to it again at luncheon on the following day.

'Mums, what does one have to do to get people out of the bin?'

'The bin? Good gracious, child, I hope that you do not anticipate your [150] father's return *here.*'

'No, no. Mr Loveday.'

'Angela, you seem to me to be totally bemused. [3] I see it was a mistake to take you with me on our little visit yesterday.'

After luncheon Angela disappeared to the library and was soon immersed [155] in the lunacy laws as represented in the encyclopedia.

She did not re-open the subject with her mother, but a fortnight later, when there was a question of taking some pheasants over to her father for his eleventh Certification Party she showed an unusual willingness to run over with them. Her mother was occupied with other interests and noticed [160] nothing suspicious.

Angela drove her small car to the asylum, and after delivering the game, [4] asked for Mr Loveday. He was busy at the time making a crown for one of his companions who expected hourly to be anointed [5] Emperor of Brazil, but he left his work and enjoyed several minutes' conversation with her. They [165] spoke about her father's health and spirits. After a time Angela remarked, 'Don't you ever want to get away?'

Mr Loveday looked at her with his gentle, blue-grey eyes. 'I've got very well used to the life, miss. I'm fond of the poor people here, and I think that

---

1	**unsympathetic** : indifferent.	4	**game** : wild animals and birds, including pheasants, hunted for sport.
2	**a looney bin** : *(colloquial)* a sort of cage full of crazy people. *(Here)* a psychiatric hospital.		
		5	**anointed** : *(here)* appointed.
3	**bemused** : confused.		

170   several of them are quite fond of me. At least, I think they would miss me if I
were to go.'
'But don't you ever think of being free again?'
'Oh yes, miss, I think of it – almost all the time I think of it.'
'What would you do if you got out? There must be *something* you would
175   sooner do than stay here.'
The old man fidgeted [1] uneasily. 'Well, miss, it sounds ungrateful, but I
can't deny I should welcome a little outing, once, before I get too old to enjoy
it. I expect we all have our secret ambitions, and there *is* one thing I often
wish I could do. You mustn't ask me what ... It wouldn't take long. But I do
180   feel that if I had done it, just for a day, an afternoon even, then I would die
quiet. I could settle down again easier, and devote myself to the poor crazed
people here with a better heart. Yes, I do feel that.'
There were tears in Angela's eyes that afternoon as she drove away.
'He *shall* have his little outing, bless him,' she said.

• •

Focus on Angela

10 a Complete the following table.

Her feelings on leaving the asylum	
Reasons why she consulted the encyclopedia	
Her reaction after talking to Mr Loveday	

b How do you think the story will develop? Work with a partner and discuss a
possible continuation of the story.

Read the next section carefully, then insert appropriate information in the chart
which follows.

---

1   **fidgeted** [fɪdʒɪtɪd] : made small nervous movements.

From that day onwards for many weeks Angela had a new purpose in life. 185
She moved about the ordinary routine of her home with an abstracted air and
an unfamiliar, reserved courtesy which greatly disconcerted Lady Moping.

'I believe the child's in love. I only pray that it isn't that uncouth [1]
Egbertson boy.'

She read a great deal in the library, she cross-examined any guests who 190
had pretensions to legal or medical knowledge, she showed extreme
goodwill to old Sir Roderick Lane-Foscote, their Member. The names
'alienist', 'barrister' or 'government official' now had for her the glamour
that formerly surrounded film actors and professional wrestlers. [2] She was a
woman with a cause, and before the end of the hunting season she had 195
triumphed. Mr Loveday achieved his liberty.

The doctor at the asylum showed reluctance but no real opposition. Sir
Roderick wrote to the Home Office. The necessary papers were signed, and
at last the day came when Mr Loveday took leave of the home where he had
spent such long and useful years. 200

His departure was marked by some ceremony. Angela and Sir Roderick
Lane-Foscote sat with the doctors on the stage of the gymnasium. Below
them were assembled everyone in the institution who was thought to be
stable enough to endure the excitement.

Lord Moping, with a few suitable expressions of regret, presented Mr 205
Loveday on behalf of the wealthier lunatics with a gold cigarette case; those
who supposed themselves to be emperors showered him with decorations
and titles of honour. The warders gave him a silver watch and many of the
non-paying inmates were in tears on the day of the presentation.

The doctor made the main speech of the afternoon. 'Remember,' he 210
remarked, 'that you leave behind you nothing but our warmest good wishes.
You are bound to us by ties that none will forget. Time will only deepen our
sense of debt to you. If at any time in the future you should grow tired of
your life in the world, there will always be a welcome for you here. Your post
will be open.' 215

A dozen or so variously afflicted lunatics hopped and skipped after him
down the drive until the iron gates opened and Mr Loveday stepped into his
freedom. His small trunk had already gone to the station; he elected to walk.
He had been reticent about his plans, but he was well provided with money,
and the general impression was that he would go to London and enjoy 220
himself a little before visiting his step-sister in Plymouth.

---

1   **uncouth** [ʌnkuːθ] : rude, impolite,   2   **wrestlers** [resləz] : fighters.
     unpleasant.

105

11 The Day of the Presentation

Who	What
Angela, Sir Roderick, the doctors	
	were assembled below the stage
	gave Mr Loveday a gold cigarette case
Those who supposed themselves to be emperors	
	gave him a silver watch
Many of the non-paying inmates	
	made the main speech
About a dozen lunatics	

12 Read the final part of the story and say if the conclusion is:

☐ amusing	☐ tragic
☐ predictable	☐ funny
☐ unexpected	☐ other…

Compare your answer/s with your partner.

It was to the surprise of all that he returned within two hours of his liberation. He was smiling whimsically, [1] a gentle, self-regarding smile of reminiscence.

'I have come back,' he informed the doctor. 'I think that now I shall be here for good.' [2]   225

'But, Loveday, what a short holiday. I'm afraid that you have hardly enjoyed yourself at all.'

'Oh yes, sir, thank you, sir, I've enjoyed myself *very much*. I'd been promising myself one little treat, all these years. It was short, sir, but *most*   230 enjoyable. Now I shall be able to settle down again to my work here without any regrets.'

Half a mile up the road from the asylum gates, they later discovered an abandoned bicycle. It was a lady's machine of some antiquity. Quite near it in the ditch lay the strangled body of a young woman, who, riding home to   235 her tea, had chanced to overtake Mr Loveday, as he strode along, musing on [3] his opportunities.

AFTER READING

13 In the story you have just read the events are narrated:

☐ chronologically   ☐ in jumbled order

---

1   **whimsically** : oddly, in a strange way.   3   **musing on** : thinking about.
2   **for good** : forever.

14 The writer has chosen to do so to:

☐ puzzle the reader

☐ let the reader understand the characters better

☐ focus on a particular character

☐ create more suspense

Discuss your choices in a group.

A Newspaper Article

15 Imagine you are a journalist. Think of a glamorous headline and use the guidelines below to write an article on Mr Loveday.

Paragraph 1 Introduce the most dramatic moments of Mr Loveday's life. Try to arouse expectation in your readers!

Paragraph 2 Include some interviews with the people at the asylum (both guests and doctors). Try to keep your readers' interest!

Paragraph 3 Conclude your article by saying what is going to happen to Mr Loveday.

Story and Plot

16 Story: the chronological sequence of events which make up a literary text.

Plot: the way in which the sequence of events is arranged and told by the author, and which develops in a sort of cause-effect chain.

The following events are given in the same order as they are put by the author in Mr Loveday's Little Outing (Plot). Number them so as to put them in chronological order and reconstruct the Story.

☐ Angela and her mother go to the Asylum.

☐ Lady Moping organises her annual garden party.

☐ Lord Moping attempts suicide.

☐ Lord Moping is taken to the mental hospital.

☐ Lady Moping occasionally visits her husband.

☐ Angela sees her father for the first time in 10 years.

☐ Angela meets Mr Loveday.

☐ Angela speaks to Mr Loveday privately.

☐ Mr Loveday is let out of the Asylum.

☐ Mr Loveday kills a young woman and goes back to the Asylum.

A Closer Look at Character-Traits

17 Complete the following table of character-traits, working with a partner.

Some words have already been inserted for you. Check in your monolingual dictionary when you have finished!

Adjective	Noun
arrogant	arrogance
shy	
mean	meanness
snobbish	
dishonest	dishonesty
stubborn	
aggressive	
frank	
generous	
sensitive	
patient	
ambitious	ambition
creative	

18 Now write down some examples using the words you have worked on.

Composing

19 Write a composition on one of the following topics.

    a The tragedy of mental disease calls for solidarity and support, both in the family and in society. Comment on this statement.

    b My last visit to a relative in hospital.

Word-File

20 Revise all the new words you have met throughout the story you have just read: highlight the words which you think will be useful for communication and insert them in the following table.

Useful Words	Meaning

The Tell-Tale Heart

by Edgar Allan Poe

Edgar Allan Poe

Edgar Allan Poe was born in January 1809, in Boston. His parents were both actors. In 1811, when Poe was two years old, his mother, Elizabeth Arnold Hopkins died of tuberculosis. He went to live with Mrs Frances Allan in Richmond (hence his name).

The house of Frances and John Allan in Richmond, Virginia,
where Poe lived for a time.

He registered at the University of Virginia in 1826 but never completed his education because of getting involved in gambling and running into debt.

He settled in Baltimore in 1832, where he spent years of poverty with his aunt and cousin, Virginia Clemm, whom he married in 1836 when she was just thirteen.

Virginia died of tuberculosis in 1847 at the age of 24. Edgar started drinking heavily, taking laudanum and probably opium.

He was found unconscious on October 3rd, 1849, in front of a voting station in Baltimore and was taken to Washington Hospital.

He died at the age of 40 on October 7th, 1849.

Main works:

MS Found in a Bottle (1833)

The Fall of the House of Usher (1839)

Tales of the Grotesque and Arabesque, from which the story here is taken (1840)

The Murders in the Rue Morgue (1841)

The Pit and the Pendulum (1842)

The Mystery of Marie Roget (1843)

The Gold Bug (1843)

The Purloined Letter (1844)

The Raven and Other Poems (1845)

The Cask of Amontillado (1846)

BEFORE READING

1 Work in a group and complete.

    a A 'vulture' is...

    b The expression 'He is a vulture' is used to indicate a person who...

Your monolingual dictionary may be helpful!

2 Look at the title and say what sort of story you expect to read.

The Tell-Tale Heart

3 Read the beginning of the story and say what:

    a the narrator is going to do.

    b idea the narrator is fighting against.

    c effects his disease has provoked.

• •

True! – nervous – very, very dreadfully nervous I had been and am; but why *will* you say that I am mad? The disease[1] had sharpened my senses[2] – not destroyed – not dulled[3] them. Above all was the sense of hearing acute. I heard all things in the heaven and in the earth. I heard many things in hell.
5   How, then, am I mad? Hearken![4] and observe how healthily – how calmly I can tell you the whole story.

• •

4 Highlight the expression/s which reveal/s the narrator's mental state and say what it/they might prove.

Read through Part 2 and use one or more words to fill in the gaps in the Summary which follows.

---

1 **disease** : sickness, illness.

2 **sharpened my senses** : improved my senses.

3 **dulled** : (*here*) weakened.

4 **Hearken** : (*archaic form*) Listen!

The Tell-Tale Heart

It is impossible to say how first the idea entered my brain; but, once conceived, it haunted [1] me day and night. Object there was none. Passion there was none. I loved the old man. He had never wronged me. He had never given me insult. For his gold I had no desire. I think it was his eye! yes, ₁₀ it was this! He had the eye of a vulture – a pale blue eye, with a film [2] over it. Whenever it fell upon me, my blood ran cold; and so by degrees – very gradually – I made up my mind to take the life of the old man, and thus [3] rid myself of the eye forever.

5 The narrator says that the idea of .... tormented him day and
.... He also says that the idea originated neither from hate,
because he .... , nor from his gold, because he ....
Then he adds that the idea actually started from .... which looked
like a vulture's eye. .... the narrator decided to get rid of the
.... forever.

6 Explain what the expression 'my blood ran cold' suggests about the narrator's
feelings when the eye fell upon him.

Read Part 3 carefully, then complete the grid which follows.

1 **haunted** : never left me.   3 **thus** : so.
2 **film** : thin membrane or covering.

15   Now this is the point. You fancy me mad. Madmen know nothing. But you should have seen *me*. You should have seen how wisely I proceeded – with what caution – with what foresight – with what dissimulation I went to work! I was never kinder to the old man than during the whole week before I killed him. And every night, about midnight, I turned the latch of his door
20 and opened it – oh, so gently! And then, when I had made an opening sufficient for my head, I put in a dark lantern, all closed, closed, so that no light shone out, and then I thrust in my head. [1] Oh, you would have laughed to see how cunningly I thrust it in! I moved it slowly – very, very slowly, so that I might not disturb the old man's sleep. It took me an hour to place my
25 whole head within the opening so far that I could see him as he lay upon his bed. Ha! – would a madman have been so wise as this? And then, when my head was well in the room, I undid the lantern cautiously – oh, so cautiously – cautiously (for the hinges [2] creaked) – I undid it just so much that a single thin ray fell upon the vulture eye. And this I did for seven long nights –
30 every night just at midnight – but I found the eye always closed; and so it was impossible to do the work; for it was not the old man who vexed me, [3] but his Evil Eye. And every morning, when the day broke, I went boldly into the chamber, and spoke courageously to him, calling him by name in a hearty [4] tone, and inquiring how he had passed the night. So you see he
35 would have been a very profound old man, indeed, to suspect that every night, just at twelve, I looked in upon him while he slept.

1 **thrust in my head** : put my head in.	3 **vexed me** : made me angry.
2 **hinges** [hɪndʒɪz] : door-joints.	4 **hearty** : enthusiastic.

7

Narrator's Comments on his Behaviour and Mental State	Lines
You fancy me mad... But you should have seen how wisely...	15-16

8 Why do you think the narrator makes such comments?

9 Why doesn't the narrator kill the old man?

10 Read Part 4 and complete the following table.

What the narrator felt upon the 8th night	
At what idea the narrator was nearly laughing	
Simile used to define the room	
What the old man shouted	

• •

Upon the eighth night I was more than usually cautious in opening the door. A watch's minute hand [1] moves more quickly than did mine. Never before that night, had I *felt* the extent of my own powers – of my sagacity. I could scarcely contain my feelings of triumph. To think that there I was,   40

1   **minute hand** : the hand of a watch indicating the minutes.

opening the door, little by little, and he not even to dream of my secret deeds or thoughts. I fairly chuckled [1] at the idea; and perhaps he heard me; for he moved on the bed suddenly, as if startled. Now you may think that I drew back – but no. His room was as black as pitch [2] with the thick darkness, (for

45 the shutters were close fastened, through fear of robbers,) and so I knew that he could not see the opening of the door, and I kept pushing it on steadily, steadily.

I had my head in, and was about to open the lantern, when my thumb slipped upon the tin fastening, and the old man sprang up in bed, crying out –

50 'Who 's there?'

• •

11 Scan through Part 5 and circle the words/expressions referring to the narrator's feelings and perceptions.

• •

I kept quite still and said nothing. For a whole hour I did not move a muscle, and in the meantime I did not hear him lie down. He was still sitting up in the bed listening; – just as I have done, night after night, hearkening to the death watches [3] in the wall.

55 Presently I heard a slight groan, and I knew it was the groan of mortal terror. It was not a groan of pain or of grief – oh, no! – it was the low stifled [4] sound that arises from the bottom of the soul when overcharged with *awe*. [5] I knew the sound well. Many a night, just at midnight, when all the world slept, it has welled up [6] from my own bosom, deepening, with its dreadful

60 echo, the terrors that distracted me. I say I knew it well. I knew what the old man felt, and pitied him, although I chuckled at heart. I knew that he had been lying awake ever since the first slight noise, when he had turned in the bed. His fears had been ever since growing upon him. He had been trying to fancy them causeless, but could not. He had been saying to himself – 'It is

65 nothing but the wind in the chimney – it is only a mouse crossing the floor', or 'it is merely a cricket [7] which has made a single chirp'. Yes, he had been

1	**chuckled** [tʃʌkəld] : laughed.	4	**stifled** [staifəld] : quiet.
2	**pitch** : black substance.	5	**awe** [ɔ:] : fear.
3	**death watches** : insects which eat wood.	6	**welled up** : developed.
		7	**cricket** : brown jumping insect.

118

trying to comfort himself with these suppositions: but he had found all in vain. *All in vain*; because Death, in approaching him had stalked[1] with his black shadow before him, and enveloped[2] the victim. And it was the mournful[3] influence of the unperceived shadow that caused him to feel – although he neither saw nor heard – to *feel* the presence of my head within the room.

70

• •

12 Answer:

    a What sort of 'groan' did the narrator often feel?

    b What did the narrator say about the old man's feelings?

    c What did the narrator think that Death had done?

13 Read Part 6 and say if the following statements are true or false. Tick appropriately, then correct the false ones.

	True	False
The narrator opened the lantern quickly		
A ray of light fell upon the old man's eye		
The old man's eye was closed		
The narrator grew quieter when he looked at the old man's eye		
The narrator heard the beating of the old man's heart		
The noise of the beating heart aroused an uncontrollable anger in the narrator		
The old man shrieked three times		
The narrator cried after killing the old man		

1   **stalked** : followed him quietly.

2   **enveloped** : wrapped, closed all around.

3   **mournful** : sad.

When I had waited a long time, very patiently, without hearing him lie down, I resolved to open a little – a very, very little crevice [1] in the lantern. So I opened it – you cannot imagine how stealthily, stealthily [2] – until, at length, a single dim ray, like the thread of the spider, shot from out the crevice and fell full upon the vulture eye.

It was open – wide, wide open – and I grew furious as I gazed upon it. I saw it with perfect distinctness – all a dull blue, with a hideous veil over it that chilled the very marrow in my bones; but I could see nothing else of the old man's face or person: for I had directed the ray as if by instinct, precisely upon the damned spot.

And now – have I not told you that what you mistake for madness is but over-acuteness of the senses? – now, I say, there came to my ears *a low, dull, quick sound, such as a watch makes when enveloped in cotton.* I knew *that* sound well, too. It was the beating of the old man's heart. It increased my fury, as the beating of a drum stimulates the soldier into courage.

But even yet I refrained and kept still. I scarcely breathed. [3] I held the lantern motionless. I tried how steadily I could maintain the ray upon the eye. Meantime the hellish tattoo [4] of the heart increased. It grew quicker and quicker, and louder and louder every instant. The old man's terror *must* have been extreme! It grew louder, I say, louder every moment! – do you mark me [5] well? I have told you that I am nervous: so I am. And now at the dead hour of the night, amid [6] the dreadful silence of that old house, so strange a noise as this excited me to uncontrollable terror. Yet, for some minutes longer I refrained and stood still. But the beating grew louder, *louder!* I thought the heart must burst. And now a new anxiety seized me – the sound would be heard by a neighbor! The old man's hour had come! With a loud yell, [7] I threw open the lantern and leaped into the room. He shrieked once – once only. In an instant I dragged him to the floor, and pulled the heavy bed over him. I then smiled gaily, to find the deed so far done. But, for many minutes, the heart beat on with a muffled [8] sound. This, however, did not vex me; it would not be heard through the wall. At length it ceased. The old man was dead. I removed the bed and examined the corpse. Yes, he was stone, stone

1 **crevice** [krevɪs] : little opening.
2 **stealthily** [stelθɪli] : quietly, in order not to be heard.
3 **I scarcely breathed** : I hardly took a breath.
4 **tattoo** : sound similar to a drum beat.
5 **do you mark me** : are you paying attention to me.
6 **amid** : in the middle of.
7 **yell** : shout.
8 **muffled** : quiet, unclear.

dead.[1] I placed my hand upon the heart and held it there many minutes. 105
There was no pulsation. He was stone dead. His eye would trouble *me* no
more.

● ●

Focus on Comparisons

14 What are the following elements compared to? Complete:

    a The ray coming from the lantern is compared to...

    b The 'low, dull, quick sound' that the narrator hears is compared to...

    c The beating of the old man's heart is compared to...

15 What is evoked by the expression 'hellish tattoo'?

16 Until this point tension has been increasing. Now it may be said it has reached a
climax. Identify it by underlining one/some sentence/s in the text.

17 The words in the table below have been taken from the next part. They are listed
in scrambled order and have been divided according to grammatical categories.
Read the gapped text and try to place them correctly.

Adjectives	Adverbs	Nouns	Verbs	Pronouns
dark	cunningly	scantlings[2]	had caught	nothing
mad	now	legs	took	his
	hastily	knocking		
		concealment		

1 **stone dead** : completely dead.   2 **scantlings** : small planks.

If still you think me .... , you will think so no longer when I describe
the wise precautions I took for the .... of the body. The night waned,[1]
110   and I worked .... , but in silence. First of all I dismembered the corpse.
I cut off the head and the arms and the .... I then .... up
three planks[2] from the flooring of the chamber, and deposited all between the
.... I then replaced the boards so cleverly, so .... , that no
human eye – not even .... – could have detected anything wrong.
115   There was .... to wash out – no stain of any kind – no blood-spot
whatever. I had been too wary for that. A tub .... all – ha! ha!
When I had made an end of these labors, it was four o'clock – still ....
as midnight. As the bell sounded the hour, there came a .... at the
street door. I went down to open it with a light heart, – for what had I
120   .... to fear?

● ●

18 Read the following section carefully, then answer the questions.

a Why did the officers go there?

b Where did the narrator pretend that the old man was?

c What happened to the narrator?

● ●

There entered three men, who introduced themselves, with perfect
suavity, as officers of the police. A shriek had been heard by a neighbor
during the night; suspicion of foul play[3] had been aroused; information had
been lodged at the police office, and they (the officers) had been deputed to
125   search the premises.

I smiled, – for *what* had I to fear? I bade the gentlemen welcome. The
shriek, I said, was my own in a dream. The old man, I mentioned, was absent
in the country. I took my visitors all over the house. I bade[4] them search –
search *well*. I led them, at length, to *his* chamber. I showed them his treasures,
130   secure, undisturbed. In the enthusiasm of my confidence, I brought chairs
into the room, and desired them *here* to rest from their fatigues, while I

---

1   **waned** : was about to end.
2   **planks** : boards, pieces of wood used
    in building.
3   **foul play** : criminal violence or
    activity that results in death.
4   **bade** : invited them.

myself, in the wild audacity of my perfect triumph, placed my own seat upon the very spot beneath which reposed the corpse of the victim.

The officers were satisfied. My *manner* had convinced them. I was singularly at ease. They sat, and while I answered cheerily, they chatted of familiar things. But, ere [1] long, I felt myself getting pale and wished them gone. My head ached, and I fancied a ringing in my ears: but still they sat and still chatted. The ringing became more distinct: – it continued and became more distinct: I talked more freely to get rid of the feeling: but it continued and gained definitiveness – until, at length, I found that the noise was *not* within my ears.

No doubt I now grew *very* pale; – but I talked more fluently, and with a heightened voice. Yet the sound increased – and what could I do? It was *a low, dull, quick sound – much such a sound as a watch makes when enveloped in cotton.* I gasped for breath – and yet the officers heard it not. I talked more quickly – more vehemently; [2] but the noise steadily increased. I arose and argued about trifles, in a high key and with violent gesticulations; but the noise steadily increased. Why *would* they not be gone? I paced [3] the floor to and fro with heavy strides, as if excited to fury by the observations of the men – but the noise steadily increased. Oh God! what *could* I do? I foamed [4] – I raved [5] – I swore! I swung the chair upon which I had been sitting, and grated it upon the boards, but the noise arose over all and continually increased. It grew louder – louder – *louder*! And still the men chatted pleasantly, and smiled. Was it possible they heard not? Almighty [6] God! – no, no! They heard! – they suspected! – they *knew*! – they were making a mockery of [7] my horror! – this I thought, and this I think. But anything was better than this agony! Anything was more tolerable than this derision! I could bear [8] those hypocritical smiles no longer! I felt that I must scream or die! – and now – again! – hark! louder! louder! louder! *louder*!

'Villains!' [9] I shrieked, 'dissemble [10] no more! I admit the deed! – tear up the planks! – here, here! – it is the beating of his hideous heart!'

1   **ere** [eər] : before.
2   **vehemently** [viːɪməntli] : with strong feeling.
3   **paced** : walked nervously.
4   **foamed** : let foam out of the mouth.
5   **raved** : spoke angrily.
6   **Almighty** : Powerful.
7   **making a mockery of** : making fun of.
8   **bear** : stand, tolerate.
9   **Villains** : criminals, awful people.
10   **dissemble** : hide the facts.

Focus on how the Narrator builds up Tension

19 Complete the following table, quoting from the text. Something has already been written for you!

The Officers	The Narrator	The Sound/Noise
were satisfied	was singularly at ease	/ /
still chatted	I felt myself getting pale My head ached	I fancied a ringing in my ears

Just a tick ✔

20 The narrator is led to confess his crime by:

☐ the fact that the policemen seem to ignore him and continue talking.

☐ the noise he hears.

☐ the fact that the policemen do not hear the noise.

Compare your choices with your classmates.

Focus on Language

21 Highlight all exclamations, words written in italics and repetitions, then say what effect you think they produce on the narrative rhythm of the story.

22 Say to what effect direct speech is used on lines 160-161.

The Tell-Tale Heart

Focus on Symbols

23 A symbol is something (a person, an animal, an object) which is used to represent an abstract idea.

Example:

A lion is the symbol of strength　　　⇨　　　something abstract

⇩

Animal which can be both seen and heard

Now work with a partner and complete:

a The vulture eye may symbolize...

b The beating heart may symbolize...

Focus on Narration and Narrator

24 In the part you have just read there is another climax. Identify it by underlining one/some sentence/s in the text.

Choose the graph which best represents the way in which the story develops.

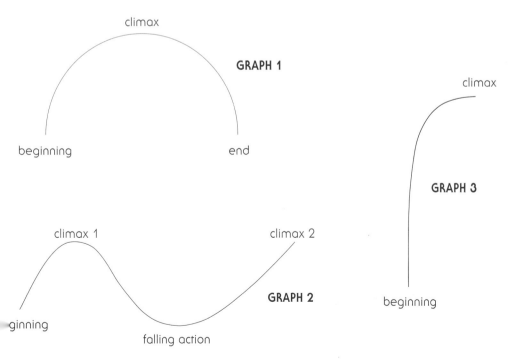

25 Write appropriate phrases to explain the headings of the graph you have chosen.

Example: beginning = the narrator starts to tell his story.

26 Tick appropriately.

   a The story is told by:

   ☐ a third person narrator

   ☐ a first person witness narrator

   ☐ a first person protagonist narrator

   ☐ a third person omniscient narrator

   b The events are filtered through the viewpoint of:

   ☐ the old man

   ☐ the author

   ☐ the narrator

Compare your choices with your classmates.

27 Work with a partner, select some of the adjectives in the box below and say how the narrator felt when:

   a the policemen arrived

   b he put the chair upon the old man's corpse

   c the noise became louder

   d he said 'I admit the deed!'

happy	scared	worried	terrified	sad	angry
proud	quiet	unhappy	self-confident	anxious	

Focus on the Title of the Story and:

28 explain the meaning of 'tell-tale'.

29 say whether 'tell tale' is used in the title as:

   ☐ a noun

   ☐ a verb

   ☐ an adjective

The Tell-Tale Heart

30 Look at the following definitions of the word 'heart' and select the one/s which best suit/s the title of the story.

    a hollow muscular organ that pumps blood through the body

    b centre of a person's thoughts and emotions

    c enthusiasm   .

    d central, innermost or most important part of something

AFTER READING

Retelling the Story

31 Write down something next to the headings below; then stand up and tell your classmates what you have written.

The .... starts with ....

....

....

....

....

It is set in ... .

....

....

....

....

First ... .

....

....

....

....

Then ... .

....

....

....

....

After that ....

....

....

....

....

Edgar Allan Poe

In the end ....
....
....
....
....

32 a Is the outcome of the story predictable/unexpected/surprising? Why?

b Is the setting of the story definite/indefinite? To what effect?

c Can *The Tell-tale Heart* be classified as a psychological/comic/grotesque/ romantic/crime/self-confession story? Why?

Word-File

33 Revise all the new words you have met throughout the story you have just read: highlight the words which you think will be useful for communication and insert them in the following table.

Useful Words	Meaning

UNIT THREE

Unforgettable
Characters

"The World is My Oyster"

Frankie Goes to Hollywood

The Robot Who Wanted to Know

by Felix Boyd

Felix Boyd

Felix Boyd is a pseudonym of Harry Harrison, who was born in 1925 in Stamford, Connecticut. Between 1943 and 1946 he served in the US Army Air Corps, after which he attended Hunter College, an art school.

In the early 1950's he frequented the Hydra Club in New York, a meeting place for the most outstanding science fiction writers.

He has travelled to Mexico, England, Italy and Denmark.

He has also written using the pseudonym of Henry M. Dempsey.

Main works:

Deathworld Trilogy: Deathworld (1960), *Deathworld 2* (1964), *Deathworld 3* (1968)

The Stainless Steel Rat (1961)

War with the Robots (1962)

Make Room! Make Room! (1966)

Planet Story (1979)

Eden Series: West of Eden (1984), *Winter in Eden* (1986), *Return to Eden* (1988)

The Planet of the Bottled Brains (1990)

Galactic Dreams (1994)

The Robot Who Wanted to Know

BEFORE READING

1 Look at the the picture and try to give a definition of the word 'robot'.

Compare your definition with your classmates.

2 Use your monolingual dictionary to check how close you got to the exact definition of the word.

Discuss the following points in a group:

3 The main difference/s between men and machines.

4 What a robot is expected to do.

5 How a robot is supposed to behave.

6 To what extent a robot may be considered as an intelligent being with feelings.

7 Whether an 'intelligent' robot may be dangerous to society.

8 Look at the title of the story and suggest what the story is about.

The Robot Who Wanted to Know

Felix Boyd

9 Listen to the beginning of the story and complete the following table.

Why Filer 13B-445-K was different from other robots	
What the robot watched intently	
What the robot told the blonde girl	

Check your answers by reading the text.

     That was the trouble with Filer 13B-445-K, he wanted to know things that he had just no business knowing. Things that *no* robot should be interested in – much less investigate. But Filer was a very different type of robot.

The trouble with the blonde in tier [1] 22 should have been warning enough
5   for him. He had hummed out [2] of the stack room [3] with a load of books, and was cutting through tier 22 when he saw her bending over for a volume on the bottom shelf.

As he passed behind her he slowed down, then stopped a few yards farther on. He watched her intently, a strange glint [4] in his metallic eyes.

---

1 **tier** [tiər]: corridor.

2 **had hummed out** : had come out.

3 **stack room** : place where books are put on shelves.

4 **glint** : sparkle indicating a particular emotion.

The Robot Who Wanted to Know

As the girl bent over her short skirt rode up to display an astonishing [10] length of nylon-clad[1] leg. That it was a singularly attractive leg should have been of no interest to a robot – yet it was. He stood there, looking, until the blonde turned suddenly and noticed his fixed attention.

'If you were human, Buster'[2], she said, 'I would slap your face for being rude. But since you are a robot, I would like to know what your little photon- [15] filled eyes[3] find so interesting?'

Without a microsecond's hesitation, Filer answered, 'Your seam[4] is crooked.'[5] Then he turned and buzzed away.

• •

10 Read Part 2 and complete the following sentences.

   a The blonde was surprised at what Filer had said because…

   b The robot had not lied because…

   c Filer was personally interested in…

   d If Filer were asked about a book he could…

   e Filer had become an expert on love because…

   f Filer had decided to implement his knowledge on love by…

• •

The blonde shook her head in wonder, straightened the offending seam, and chalked up[6] another credit to the honour of electronics. [20]

She would have been very surprised to find out what Filer had been looking at. He *had* been staring at her leg. Of course he hadn't lied when he answered her – since he was incapable of lying – but he had been looking at a lot more than the crooked seam. Filer was facing a problem that no other robot had ever faced before. [25]

Love, romance, and sex were fast becoming a passionate interest for him.

That this interest was purely academic goes without saying, yet it was still an interest. It was the nature of his work that first aroused his curiosity about the realm of Venus.

1	**nylon-clad** : wearing tights or stockings.	4	**seam** : the dark line on tights or stockings.
2	**Buster** : informal way of addressing a man.	5	**crooked** : not straight.
		6	**chalked up** : mentally added.
3	**photon-filled eyes** : eyes full of units of light.		

30   A Filer is an amazingly intelligent robot and there aren't very many being manifactured. You will find them only in the greatest libraries, dealing with only the largest and most complex collections. To call them simply librarians is to demean all librarians and to call their work simple. Of course very little intelligence is required to shelf books or stamp cards, but this sort of work
35   has long been handled by robots that are little more than wheeled IBM machines. The cataloguing of human information has always been an incredibly complex task. The Filer robots were the ones who finally inherited this job. It rested easier on their metallic shoulders than it ever had on the rounded ones of human librarians.

40   Besides a complete memory, Filer had other attributes that are usually connected with the human brain. Abstract connections for one thing. If he was asked for books on one subject, he could think of related books in other subjects that might be referred to. He could take a suggestion, pyramid [1] it into a category, then produce tactile results in the form of a mountain of
45   books.

(...)

In addition to all gleaming new microfiles, he had access to tons of ancient printed-on-paper books that dated back for centuries.

Filer had found *his* interest in the novels of that by-gone [2] time.

50   At first he was confused by all the reference to *love* and *romance*, as well as the mental and physical suffering that seemed to accompany them. He could find no satisfactory or complete definition of the terms and was intrigued. [3] Intrigue led to interest and finally absorption. Unknown to the world at large, he became an authority on love.

55   Very early in his interest, Filer realized that this was the most delicate of all human institutions. He therefore kept his researches a secret and the only records he kept were in the capacious circuits of his brain. Just about the same time he discovered that he could do research, *in vivo*, to supplement the facts in his books. This happened when he found a couple locked in embrace
60   in the zoology section.

Quickly stepping back into the shadows, Filer had turned up the gain [4] on his audio pick-up. [5] The resulting dialogue he heard was dull to say the least. A sort of wasted shadow of the love lyrics he knew from his books. This comparison was interesting and enlightening.

1	**pyramid** : arrange.		4	**gain** : amplifier.
2	**by-gone** : past.		5	**audio pick-up** : microphone.
3	**intrigued** [ıntriːgd] : curious.			

The Robot Who Wanted to Know

After that he listened to male-female conversations whenever he had the 65
opportunity. He also tried to observe women from the viewpoint of men, and
vice versa. This is what had led him to the lower-limb observation in tier 22.

It also led him to his ultimate folly.

. . . .

11 Read Part 3 and say what:

  a the 'un-robot thought' consisted of.

  b the sentence 'breaking down the barrier between himself and the mysteries of romance' might mean.

  c revealed Filer's disguise while he was going to the party.

  d Filer did immediately after entering the ballroom.

. . . .

A researcher sought his aid a few weeks later and fumbled out[1] a thick
pile of reference notes. A card slid from the notes and fell unnoticed to the 70
floor. Filer picked it up and handed it back to the man who put it away with
mumbled thanks.

(…)

The card had been an invitation to a masquerade ball. He was well
acquainted with this type of entertainment – it was stock-in-trade for his 75
dusty novels. People went to them disguised as various romantic figures.

Why couldn't a robot go, disguised as people?

Once the idea was fixed in his head there was no driving it out. It was an
un-robot thought and a completely un-robot action. Filer had a glimmering[2]
for the first time that he was breaking down the barrier between himself and 80
the mysteries of romance. This only made him more eager to go. And of
course he did.

(…)

The night finally arrived and he left the library late with what looked like
a package of books and of course wasn't. No one noticed him enter the patch 85
of trees on the library grounds. If they had, they would certainly never have
connected him with the elegant gentleman who swept out of the far side a
few moments later. Only the empty wrapping paper bore mute evidence of
the disguise.

---

1 **fumbled out** : clumsily passed.   2 **glimmering** : a certain idea.

90   Filer's manner in his new personality was all that might be expected of a superior robot who has studied a role to perfection. He swept up the stairs to the hall, three at a time, and tendered his invitation with a flourish. Once inside he headed straight for the bar and threw down three glasses of champagne, right through a plastic tube to a tank in his thorax. Only then did

95   he let his eye roam [1] over the assembled beauties. It was a night for love.

• •

12 Listen to Part 4 and decide whether the following statements are true or false, by putting a ✓ in the right column:

	True	False
Filer was attracted to all the women in the room		
Filer was acting in memory of all heroes of forgotten books		
Carol was enjoying the party		
Carol was good-looking		
Carol was poor		
Carol could not resist the odd gleam in Filer's eyes		

Correct the false statements by reading the text.

• •

    And of all the women in the room, there was only one he had eyes for. Filer could see instantly that she was the belle of the ball and the only one to approach. Could he do anything else in memory of 50,000 heroes of those long-forgotten books?

100   Carol Ann van Damm was bored as usual. Her face was disguised, but no mask could hide the generous contours of her bosom and flanks. All her usual suitors [2] were there, dancing attendance behind their dominoes, [3]

---

1   **roam** : move freely.
2   **suitors** : men hoping to marry certain women.
3   **dominoes** : half masks.

lusting after[1] her youth and her father's money. It was all too familiar and she had trouble holding back her yawns.

Until the pack was courteously but irrevocably pushed aside by the wide   105
shoulders of the stranger. He was like a lion among wolves as he swept through them and faced her.

'This *is* our dance,' he said in a deep voice rich with meaning. Almost automatically she took the proferred hand, unable to resist this man with the strange gleam in his eyes. In a moment they were waltzing and it was   110
heaven. His muscles were like steel yet he was light and graceful as a god.

• •

13 Read Part 5 carefully and write down the reactions of:

  a Carol at hearing Filer's words.

  b Carol after kissing Filer.

  c Carol at realising that Filer was a robot.

  d Filer at hearing the words 'you're nothing but a robot'.

• •

'Who are you?' she whispered.

'Your prince, come to take you away from all this,' he murmured in her ear.

'You talk like a fairytale,' she laughed.   115

'This is a fairytale, and you are the heroine'.

His words struck fire from her brain and she felt the thrill of an electric current sweep through her. It had, just a temporary short circuit. While his lips murmured the words she had wanted to hear all her life into her ear, his magic feet led her through the great doors on to the balcony. Once there   120
words blended with action and hot lips burned against hers. 102 degrees to be exact, that was what the thermostat was set at.

'Please,' she breathed, weak with this new passion, 'I must sit down.' He sat next to her, her hands in his soft yet vice-like grip. They talked the words that only lovers know until a burst of music drew her attention.   125

'Midnight,' she breathed. 'Time to unmask, my love.' Her mask dropped off, but he of course did nothing. 'Come, come,' she said. 'You must take your mask off too.'

---

  1   **lusting after** : desiring.

It was a command and of course as a robot he had to obey. With a flourish
130 he pulled off his face.

Carol Ann screamed first, then burned with anger.

'What sort of scheme is this, you animated tin can? Answer.'

'It was love, dear one. Love that brought me here tonight and sent me to
your arms.' The answer was true enough, though Filer couched [1] it in the
135 terms of his disguise.

When the soft words of her darling came out of the harsh mouth of the
electronic speaker, Carol Ann screamed again. She knew she had been made
a fool of.

'Who sent you here like this, answer. What is the meaning of this disguise,
140 answer. ANSWER! ANSWER! you articulated pile of cams and rods!' [2]

Filer tried to sort out the questions and answer them one at a time, but she
gave him no time to speak.

'It's the filthiest trick of all time, sending you here disguised as a man.
You a robot. A nothing. A two-legged IBM machine with a victrola [3] attached.
145 Making believe you're a man when you're nothing but a robot.'

Suddenly Filer was on his feet, the words crackling and mechanical from
his speaker.

'I'm a robot.'

The soft voice of love was gone and replaced by that of mechanical
150 despair. Thought chased [4] thought through the whirling electronic circuits of
his brain and they were all the same thought.

I'm a robot – a robot – I must have forgotten I was a robot – what can a
robot be doing here with a woman – a robot can't kiss a woman – a woman
can't love a robot – yet she said she loved me – yet I'm a robot – a robot ...

155 With a mechanical shudder he turned from the girl and clanked [5] away.
With each step his steel fingers plucked at his clothes and plastic flesh until
they came away in shards [6] and pieces. Fragments of cloth marked his trail
away from the woman and within a hundred paces he was as steel-naked as
the day he was built. Through the garden and down to the street he went, the
160 thoughts in his head going in ever tighter circles.

---

1 **couched** : said.

2 **cams and rods** : mechanical parts.

3 **victrola** : record-player.

4 **chased** : followed.

5 **clanked** : moved producing a metallic sound.

6 **shards** : broken bits.

The Robot Who Wanted to Know

It was uncontrolled feedback and soon his body followed his brain. His legs went faster, his motors whirled more rapidly, and the central lubrication pump in his thorax churned[1] like a mad thing.

Then, with a single metallic screech, he raised both arms and plunged forward. His head hit a corner of a stair and the granite point thrust into the 165 thin casing.[2] Metal grounded to metal and all the complex circuits that made up his brain were instantly discharged.

Robot Filer 13B-445-K was quite dead.

• •

14 a How did Filer feel when he left the party?

  b What caused Filer to be 'quite dead'?

15 Say how you expect the story to end. Then continue reading and check your predictions!

16 Read the conclusion of the story and say/explain:

  a what the matter with Filer was, according to the second mechanic.

  b the double meaning of the sentence 'You could almost say he died of a broken heart'.

• •

That was what the report read that the mechanic sent in the following day. Not dead, but permanently impaired, to be disposed of. Yet, strangely 170 enough, that wasn't what the mechanic said when he examined the metallic corpse.

A second mechanic had helped in the examination. It was he who had spun off the bolts and pulled out the damaged lubrication pump.

'Here's the trouble,' he had announced. 'Malfunction in the pump. Piston 175 broke, jammed[3] the pump, the knees locked from lack of oil – then the robot fell and shorted out his brain.'

The first mechanic wiped grease off his hands and examined the faulty pump. Then he looked from it to the gaping hole in the chest.

---

1 **churned** : moved.   3 **jammed** : totally blocked.

2 **casing** : covering.

180 'You could almost say he died of a broken heart.'

They both laughed and he threw the pump into the corner with all the other cracked, dirty, broken and discarded machinery.

Guided Interpretation

17 Fill in the gaps.

Filer is too .... and sensitive to be a good .... but he is, on the other hand, made of .... components and that is the .... why he is not .... by mankind.

As a consequence Filer feels like an ....

The Robot Who Wanted to Know

AFTER READING

Retelling the story

18 Write a summary of the story next to the headings below, then stand up and tell your classmates what you have written.

The .... starts ....
....
....
....
....

It is set in ... .
....
....
....
....

First ... .
....
....
....
....

Then ... .
....
....
....
....

After that ... .
....
....
....
....

An Alternative Outcome

19 Did you like the end of the story? Why/why not?

20 Think of another possible ending for the story and write it in your exercise-book, then read it aloud to your class.

Over to You

21 Do you think mixing electronics and romance leads to positive achievements?

22 Who is actually responsible for Filer's position in society?

23 Would you classify the story you have just read as:

- [ ] a thriller
- [ ] an attack against science
- [ ] an attack against man's abuse of science
- [ ] a romantic story
- [ ] a story with a moral
- [ ] a humorous story

Discuss your answers with your classmates.

Word-File

24 Revise all the new words you have met throughout the story you have just read: highlight the words which you think will be useful for communication and insert them in the following table.

Useful Words	Meaning

Composing

25 Write a composition on the following topic:

'Different figures of social outcasts in the books/films I have read/seen.'

The Science Fiction Story

CROSS-CURRICULAR DATA

The Science Fiction Story

The term science-fiction was coined by William Wilson in 1851, but forerunners of this literary genre can be found in *Republic* by Plato, *Gulliver's Travels* by J. Swift and in the works of J. Verne.

It is relevant what Hugo Gernsback (1884-1967) wrote in the US sci-fi [1] magazine *Amazing Stories* in 1926 to define the literary genre:

> '...in which speculations about the future is satire about the present in disguise, satire which covers a wide range from politics to sex, to subliminal advertising.'

In the 20th century the US pulp-magazine tradition of science fiction produced such writers as Arthur C. Clarke, Isaac Asimov, Robert Heinlein, and Frank Herbert; a consensus of 'pure storytelling" and traditional values was disrupted by writers associated with the British magazine *New Worlds* (Brian Aldiss, Michael Moorcock, J. G. Ballard) and by younger US writers (Joanna Russ, Ursula Le Guin, Thomas Disch, Gene Wolfe) who used the form for serious literary purposes and for political and sexual radicalism.

The main sources of inspiration are nuclear power, space exploration, computer science and medical discoveries. Often taking its ideas and concerns from current ideas in science and the social sciences, science fiction aims to shake up standard perceptions of reality.

Early science fiction stories are based on the impact that scientific and technological discoveries have on man's future and fall into two main categories:

1 The dangers that man may have to face and his possible future annihilation if present technologies are carried further.

2 Man's possibility to go beyond the limits of the human body and to acquire some of the positive qualities of machines.

---

1   **sci-fi** : (*colloquial*) abbreviation for science fiction.

The Science Fiction Story

It can be said that both the cinema and television have contributed to the success of the genre: films like *2001: A Space Odyssey* and *Star Wars* are just some examples.

Even though writers of science fiction project their fears in different worlds, the problems remain the same: evil, good, love, hate, anguish, madness, etc.

In the 1980s the 'cyberpunk' [1] school spread from the US, spearheaded by William Gibson and Bruce Sterling (1954-).

Outstanding Works:

The Time Machine (1895) by H.G. Wells: about the use of time-travelling as a dimension to get a new view of the present day.

The War of the Worlds (1898) by H.G. Wells: about an imaginary Martian invasion of the earth.

The Machine Stops (1909) by E.M. Forster: which shows a world where machines are in control.

The Martian Chronicles (1950) by R. Bradbury: on the attempts of Earth people to colonise Mars.

I, Robot (1950) by Isaac Asimov: a collection of short stories by which the writer revolutionised the traditional belief which associated robots with evil monsters.

Neuromancer (1984) by William Gibson: a novel in which the writer used the word "Cyberspace" for the first time to define a VR world.

Note down:

1 the forerunners of science fiction.

2 the main sources of inspiration.

3 how science fiction stories can be classified.

4 what is revolutionary in *I, Robot* (1950).

---

1   **cyberpunk** : a style of science fiction featuring urban counter-culture in a world of high technology and virtual reality (VR).

The Hobbyist

by Frederic Brown

Frederic Brown

Frederic Brown was born in 1906 in Cincinnati, Ohio, into a lower middle-class family. He started to work in a funfair and then as a clerk in a firm.

He attended Ohio University in 1926 and then went to Hanover College, Indiana. However, he did not graduate.

He married Helen Brown in 1929 and in 1936 he sold his first detective short stories. He divorced in 1947 and married Elizabeth Charlies in 1948.

He died in 1972 as a result of a lung disease.

Main works:

The Fabulous Clipjoint (1947)

Murder Can Be Fun (1948)

What Mad Universe (1949)

Martian Go Home (1955)

The Five-Day Nightmare (1962)

The Best of Frederic Brown, a collection of stories (1977)

BEFORE READING

1 Look at the following picture and the title and try to predict what the story is about.

The Hobbyist

Compare your predictions with your classmates.

2 Listen to the beginning of the story and complete the following table.

Setting	
Characters involved	
What rumour one of the characters heard	
What the 'customer' was offered	

Check your answers by reading the text.

Frederic Brown

    ''I heard a rumor,' Sangstrom said, 'to the effect that you ...' He turned his head and looked about him to make absolutely sure that he and the druggist were alone in the tiny prescription pharmacy. The druggist was a gnomelike, gnarled [1] little man who could have been any age from fifty to a hundred.

5 They were alone, but Sangstrom dropped his voice just the same. '... to the effect that you have a completely undetectable poison.'

The druggist nodded. He came around the counter and locked the front door of the shop, then walked toward a doorway behind the counter. 'I was about to take a coffee break,' he said. 'Come with me and have a cup.'

• •

3 Read the beginning of the story again and try to guess the meaning of the words listed in the table below, by referring to the context in which they are used.

Check your guesses in your monolingual dictionary afterwards.

Word	Your Guess	Dictionary Definition
rumor		
druggist		
prescription		
pharmacy		
poison		

Read Part 2 carefully, then do the activity which follows.

• •

10   Sangstrom followed him around the counter and through the doorway to a back room ringed [2] by shelves of bottles from floor to ceiling. The druggist plugged in an electric percolator, [3] found two cups and put them on a table that had a chair on either side of it. He motioned Sangstrom to one of the

---

1   **gnarled** [nɑːld] : wrinkled, bent and twisted.

2   **ringed** : surrounded.

3   **percolator** : machine used to prepare coffee.

chairs and took the other himself. 'Now,' he said. 'Tell me. Whom do you
want to kill, and why?'   15

'Does it matter?' Sangstrom asked. 'Isn't it enough that I pay for ...'

The druggist interrupted him with an upraised hand. 'Yes, it matters. I
must be convinced that you deserve what I can give you. Otherwise ...' He
shrugged. [1]

'All right,' Sangstrom said. 'The *whom* is my wife. The *why...*'   20

He started the long story. Before he had quite finished the percolator had
completed its task and the druggist briefly interrupted to get the coffee for
them. Sangstrom concluded his story.

The little druggist nodded. 'Yes, I occasionally dispense an undetectable
poison. I do so freely; I do not charge [2] for it, if I think the case is deserving. I 25
have helped many murderers.'

'Fine,' Sangstrom said. 'Please give it to me then.'

The druggist smiled at him. 'I already have. By the time the coffee was
ready I had decided that you deserved it. It was, as I said, free. But there is a
price for the antidote.' [3]   30

4 a What sort of story might Sangstrom have told the druggist?

b How do you think Sangstrom will react to the druggist's revelation.

c Sangstrom has to decide what to do next. If you were Sangstrom, what would
your decision be?

Discuss your answers in your class.

---

1 **shrugged** : raised and lowered his
   shoulders.

2 **charge** : ask money.

3 **antidote** : substance which is used to
   prevent a poison from acting on a
   person.

Frederic Brown

Read to the end of the story, then do the activities which follow.

• •

Sangstrom turned pale. But he had anticipated – not this, but the possibility of a double cross [1] or some form of blackmail. [2] He pulled a pistol from his pocket.

The little druggist chuckled. [3] 'You daren't use that. Can you find the
35 antidote ...' he waved at the shelves '... among those thousands of bottles? Or would you find a faster, more virulent poison? Or if you think I'm bluffing, that you are not really poisoned, go ahead and shoot. You'll know the answer within three hours when the poison starts to work.'

'How much for the antidote?' Sangstrom growled. [4]
40 'Quite reasonable, a thousand dollars. After all, a man must live; even if his hobby is preventing murders, there's no reason why he shouldn't make money at it, is there?'

Sangstrom growled and put the pistol down, but within reach, and took out his wallet.

45 Maybe after he had the antidote, he'd still use that pistol. He counted out a thousand dollars in hundred-dollar bills and put them on the table.

The druggist made no immediate move to pick them up. He said, 'And one other thing – for your wife's safety and mine. You will write a confession of your intention – your former intention, I trust – to murder your wife. Then
50 you will wait till I go out and mail it to a friend of mine on the homicide detail. He'll keep it as evidence [5] in case you ever *do* decide to kill your wife. Or me, for that matter.

'When that is in the mail it will be safe for me to return here and give you the antidote. I'll get you paper and pen. Oh, one other thing – although I do
55 not absolutely insist on it. Please help spread the word about my undetectable poison, will you? One never knows, Mr. Sangstrom. The life you save, if you have any enemies, just might be your own.'

---

1   **double cross** : trick, betrayal.

2   **blackmail** : action of threatening a
     person to get money.

3   **chuckled** [tʃʌkld] : laughed quietly.

4   **growled** : made a rough sound.

5   **evidence** : proof.

The Hobbyist

5 a Explain the meaning of the final sentence 'The life you save, if you have any enemies, just might be your own.'

b Work with a partner and complete the following sentences:

1 Sangstrom had foreseen...

2 The druggist told Sangstrom that the poison would...

3 The druggist asked Sangstrom for...

4 Sangstrom thought he could use his pistol...

5 The druggist made Sangstrom write...

6 Sangstrom would be given the antidote...

6 Use the words in the box below to complete the following summary of the story.

publicise	use	druggist	friend	murder	be able
poison	help	afraid	coffee	to pay	poisoned
	pocket	being killed		confession	

One day, a man called Sangstrom went to a .... 's because he wanted to buy some .... to kill his wife. The druggist offered him some .... , then told Sangstrom that he had .... him. Sangstrom took a pistol out of his .... The druggist showed that he was not .... because without his .... Sangstrom would not .... to survive and find the right antidote among the thousands of bottles in the pharmacy. Then the druggist asked Sangstrom .... 1000 dollars for the antidote. To avoid .... , the druggist also made Sangstrom write a .... which he would send to a .... of his and which he would .... in case Sangstrom tried to .... either his wife or the druggist.

Finally, the druggist asked him to .... his poison.

7 Explain why the title of the story is/isn't appropriate. Suggest a few alternative titles.

Frederic Brown

Over to You

8 Why do you think the druggist asked Sangstrom to publicise his poison?

9 Do you think that the end of the story is surprising/predictable/unexpected/ moving/inconsistent? Give reasons for your choice/s.

10 What is your opinion of the story? Do you like/dislike it? Why?

You may support your answer by ticking one or more of the following reasons:

☐ The story is too unrealistic.

☐ There is not much action.

☐ The plot is intriguing.

☐ The topic is rather boring.

☐ The story has a lot of suspense.

☐ There are no characters I can identify with.

☐ Other.

Compare your answers with your classmates.

Word-File

11 Revise all the new words you have met throughout the story you have just read: highlight the words which you think will be useful for communication and insert them in the following table.

Useful Words	Meaning

The Veiled Lady

by Agatha Christie

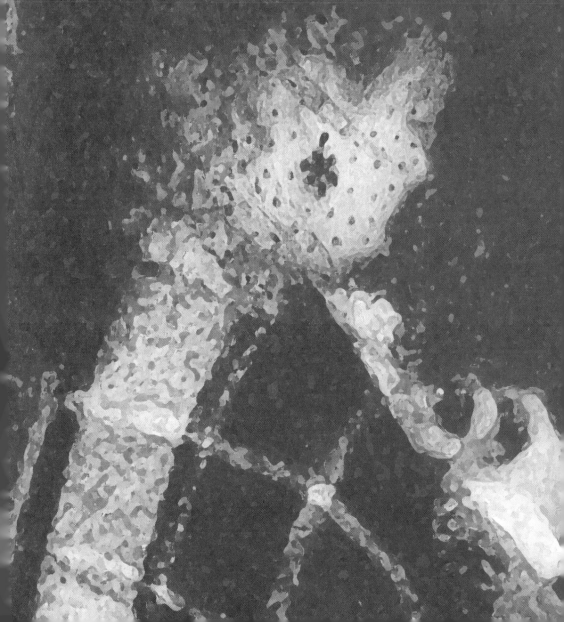

Agatha Christie

Agatha Christie was born in September 1890 in Torquay, Devonshire. She was the daughter of Frederick Alvah Miller and Clare Boehmer.

She married Archibald Christie, an English officer, in 1914, and worked as a Red Cross nurse at Torquay Hospital. Her daughter Rosalind was born in 1919.

In 1926, after discovering that her husband was having an affair with another woman she disappeared. She was found after a ten-day nationwide hunt in a health spa in Harrogate, Yorkshire. She divorced in 1928.

In 1930 she married Sir Max Mallowan, an archaeologist. Her journeys to the Middle East with him provided the background to novels such as *Death on the Nile*.

After the outburst of World War II in 1939 she worked at University College Hospital in London.

The first performance of *The Mousetrap* took place in 1952 at The Ambassador Theatre in London. It is still playing now, being the longest-running play in the West End.

Dame Agatha Christie, the prolific writer, died in 1976 in her country cottage near Oxford while murmuring 'I'm joining my Maker'.

Main works:

The Mysterious Affair at Styles (1920)	*Why Didn't They Ask Evans* (1934)
The Murder of Roger Ackroyd (1926)	*The ABC Murders* (1936)
The Murder at the Vicarage (1930)	*Death on the Nile* (1938)
Murder on the Orient Express (1934)	*Ten Little Niggers* (1939)

The Writer and her Creations

Agatha Christie is famous throughout the world as the Queen of Detective Fiction: she wrote seventy-six detective stories and novels, which have been translated into many different languages and have sold millions of copies!

Her main achievement was the creation of three outstanding detectives: Hercule Poirot, Miss Marple and Mr Parker Pyne.

Hercule Poirot was the very first detective she created: Belgian, short and bald, with a black waxed moustache. He is the sort of self-confident, often intractable man who is willing to solve the most mysterious cases in the name of justice. He is often helped by his less capable friend, Captain Hastings, who narrates his adventures.

Her second creation was Miss Marple: an old spinster naturally inclined to solve complex cases, but unwilling to leave her village.

Mr Parker Pyne is her third creation: a sort of Father Brown whose main concern is for the human heart and the establishment of peace and harmony.

Complete the following tables:

First Detective	
Name	
Nationality	
Physical features	
Personality	

Second Detective	
Name	
Age	
Natural flair	
Unwilling to	

Agatha Christie

Third Detective	
Who he resembles	
Main interest	

BEFORE READING

1 Look at the following picture and title of the story and say what you expect to read about.

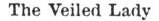

The Veiled Lady

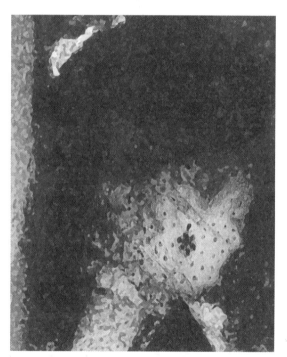

Auguste Renoir, 'Jeune Femme à la voilette' (about 1875).

2 Read the beginning of the story and say:

   a who the 'I' narrator is.

   b why Poirot is dissatisfied.

   c why the robbery in Bond Street is not in Poirot's own line.

The Veiled Lady

I had noticed that for some time Hercule Poirot had been growing increasingly dissatisfied and restless. We had had no interesting cases of late; nothing on which my little friend could exercise his keen wits and remarkable powers of deduction. This July morning he flung down [1] the newspaper with an impatient 'Tchah!' – a favourite exclamation of his which sounded exactly like a cat sneezing.

'They fear me, Hastings – the criminals of your England, they fear me! When the cat is there, the little mice, they come no more to the cheese!'

'I don't suppose the greater part of them even know of your existence,' I said, laughing.

Poirot looked at me reproachfully. He always imagines that the whole world is thinking and talking of Hercule Poirot. He had certainly made a name for himself in London, but I could hardly believe that his existence struck [2] terror into the criminal world.

'What about that daylight robbery of jewels in Bond Street the other day?' I asked.

'A neat *coup*,' said Poirot approvingly, 'though not in my line. [3] *Pas definesse, seulement de l'audace*! A man with a loaded cane [4] smashes the plate-glass window of a jeweller's shop and grabs [5] a number of precious stones. Worthy citizens immediately seize [6] him; a policeman arrives. He is caught red-handed [7] with the jewels on him. He is marched off to the police station, and then it is discovered that the stones are paste. [8] He has passed the real ones to a confederate – one of the aforementioned worthy citizens. He will go to prison – true; but when he comes out, there will be a nice little fortune awaiting him. Yes, not badly imagined. But I could do better than that. Sometimes, Hastings, I regret that I am of such a moral disposition. To work against the law, it would be pleasing, for a change.'

'Cheer up, Poirot. You know you are unique in your own line.'

'But what is there on hand in my own line?'

I picked up the paper. 'Here's an Englishman mysteriously done to death in Holland,' I said.

---

1 **flung down** : threw down angrily.

2 **struck** : caused, created.

3 **not in my line** : not of interest to me.

4 **cane** : walking stick.

5 **grabs** : takes quickly.

6 **seize** : catch.

7 **red-handed** : while committing the crime.

8 **paste** : artificial gems.

'They always say that – and later they find that he ate the tinned fish and that his death is perfectly natural.'

'Well, if you're determined to grouse!'[1]

• •

3 Read Part 2 carefully and complete the following table:

The Veiled Lady	
Name	
Hair	
Eyes	
Voice	
Social class	
Who she is engaged to	
Why she dare not confess all to the Duke	

• •

35   '*Tiens!*'' said Poirot, who had strolled[2] across to the window. 'Here in the street is what they call in novels 'a heavily veiled lady.' She mounts the steps; she rings the bell – she comes to consult us. Here is a possibility of something interesting. When one is as young and pretty as that one, one does not veil the face except for a big affair.'

40   A minute later our visitor was ushered in.[3] As Poirot had said, she was indeed heavily veiled. It was impossible to distinguish her features until she raised her veil of black Spanish lace.[4] Then I saw that Poirot's intuition had been right; the lady was extremely pretty, with fair hair and large blue eyes. From the costly simplicity of her attire, I deduced at once that she belonged

45 to an upper stratum of society.

---

1 **grouse** : complain, grumble.	4 **lace** : delicate fabric with ornamental openwork design of threads.
2 **strolled** : walked slowly.	
3 **ushered in** : let in, shown in.	

The Veiled Lady

'Monsieur Poirot,' said the lady in a soft, musical voice, 'I am in great trouble. I can hardly believe that you can help me, but I have heard such wonderful things of you that I come literally as a last hope to beg you to do the impossible.'

'The impossible, it pleases me always,' said Poirot. 'Continue, I beg of you, mademoiselle.'

Our fair guest hesitated.

'But you must be frank,' added Poirot. 'You must not leave me in the dark on any point.'

'I will trust you,' said the girl suddenly. 'You have heard of Lady Millicent Castle Vaughan?'

I looked up with keen interest. The announcement of Lady Millicent's engagement to the young Duke of Southshire had appeared a few days previously. She was, I knew, the fifth daughter of an impecunious [1] Irish peer, and the Duke of Southshire was one of the best matches in England.

'I am Lady Millicent,' continued the girl. 'You may have read of my engagement. I should be one of the happiest girls alive, but, oh, Monsieur Poirot, I am in terrible trouble! There is a man, a horrible man – his name is Lavington; and he – I hardly know how to tell you. There was a letter I wrote – I was only sixteen at the time; and he – he –'

'A letter that you wrote to this Mr. Lavington?'

'Oh, *no* – not to him! To a young soldier – I was very fond of him – he was killed in the war.'

'I understand,' said Poirot kindly.

'It was a foolish letter, an indiscreet letter, but indeed, Monsieur Poirot, nothing more. But there are phrases in it which – which might bear a different interpretation.'

'I see,' said Poirot. 'And this letter has come into the possession of Mr. Lavington?'

'Yes, and he threatens, unless I pay him an enormous sum of money, a sum that it is quite impossible for me to raise, to send it to the Duke.'

'The dirty swine!' I exclaimed. 'I beg your pardon, Lady Millicent.'

'Would it not be wiser to confess all to your future husband?'

'I dare not, Monsieur Poirot. The Duke is a very jealous man, suspicious and prone to believe the worst. I might as well break off my engagement at once.'

---

1   **impecunious** [ɪmpɪkjuːnɪəs] : penniless, without money.

161

'Dear, dear,' said Poirot with an expressive grimace. [1] 'And what do you want me to do, milady?'

'I thought perhaps that I might ask Mr Lavington to call upon you. I would tell him that you were empowered by me to discuss the matter. Perhaps you could reduce his demands.'

'What sum does he mention?'

'Twenty thousand pounds – an impossibility. I doubt if I could raise even a thousand.'

'You might perhaps borrow the money on the prospect of your coming marriage – but, *eh bien*, it is repugnant to me that you should pay! No, the ingenuity of Hercule Poirot shall defeat your enemies! Send me this Mr. Lavington. Is he likely to bring the letter with him?'

The girl shook her head.

'I do not think so. He is very cautious.'

'I suppose there is no doubt that he really has it?'

'He showed it to me when I went to his house.'

'You went to his house? That was very imprudent, milady.'

'Was it? I was so desperate. I hoped my entreaties [2] might move him.'

'Oh, *la la*! The Lavingtons of this world are not moved by entreaties! He would welcome them as showing how much importance you attached to the document. Where does he live, this fine gentleman?'

'At Buona Vista, Wimbledon. I went there after dark' – Poirot groaned [3] – 'I declared that I would inform the police in the end, but he only laughed in a horrid, sneering [4] manner. "By all means, my dear Lady Millicent, do so if you wish," he said.'

'Yes, it is hardly an affair for the police,' murmured Poirot.

'"But I think you will be wiser than that," he said. "See, here is your letter – in this little Chinese Puzzle box!" He held it so that I could see. I tried to snatch [5] at it, but he was too quick for me. With a horrid smile he folded it up and replaced it in the little wooden box. "It will be quite safe here, I assure you" he said, "and I keep the box itself in such a clever place that you would never find it." My eyes turned to the small wall safe and he shook his head and laughed. "I have a better safe than that," he said. Oh, he was odious! Do you think you can help me?'

'Have faith in Papa Poirot. I will find a way.'

---

1 **grimace** [grɪməs] : expression on the face expressing pain and disgust.

2 **entreaties** : earnest requests.

3 **groaned** : made a deep, sad sound.

4 **sneering** : unkind, rude.

5 **snatch** : grab, seize.

The Veiled Lady

4 Fill in this table.

When the letter was written	
The addressee	
Who has kept the letter	
Where the letter is hidden	
What Mr Lavington is threatening	
How much money Mr Lavington is asking for	

5 Read Part 3 and say if the following statements are true or false.

	True	False
The case appears difficult to Hastings		
Lavington wants the money by Monday		
Poirot does not want Lavington to think of him as a capable man		
Poirot and Hastings take some tools with them when they go to Lavington's house		
Poirot sees Lavington's house for the first time		
The box is in the study		

Correct the false statements.

These reassurances were all very well, I thought, as Poirot gallantly ushered his fair client down the stairs, but it seemed to me that we had a tough nut to crack. I said as much to Poirot when he returned. He nodded
120 ruefully. [1]

'Yes – the solution does not leap to the eye. He has the whip hand, this Mr. Lavington. For the moment I do not see how we are to circumvent him.'

Mr. Lavington duly called on us that afternoon. Lady Millicent had spoken truly when she described him as an odious man. I felt a positive
125 tingling [2] in the end of my foot, so keen was I to kick him down the stairs.

He was blustering [3] and overbearing in manner, laughed Poirot's gentle suggestions to scorn, and generally showed himself as master of the situation. I could not help feeling that Poirot was hardly appearing at his best. He looked discouraged and crestfallen. [4]

130 'Well, gentlemen,' said Lavington as he took up his hat, 'we don't seem to be getting much farther. The case stands like this: I'll let the Lady Millicent off cheap, as she is such a charming young lady. We'll say eighteen thousand. I'm off to Paris today – a little piece of business to attend to over there. I shall be back on Tuesday. Unless the money is paid by Tuesday evening, the letter
135 goes to the Duke. Don't tell me Lady Millicent can't raise the money. Some of her gentlemen friends would be only too willing to oblige such a pretty woman with a loan – if she goes about it the right way.'

I took a step forward, but Lavington had wheeled out of the room as he finished his sentence.

140 'Something has got to be done. You seem to be taking this lying down, Poirot,' I cried.

'You have an excellent heart, my friend – but your grey cells are in a deplorable condition. I have no wish to impress Mr. Lavington with my capabilities. The more pusillanimous [5] he thinks me, the better.'

145 'Why?'

'It is curious,' murmured Poirot reminiscently, 'that I should have uttered a wish to work against the law just before Lady Millicent arrived!'

'You are going to burgle his house while he is away?' I gasped. [6]

---

1 **ruefully** : showing good-humoured regret.

2 **tingling** : a slight pricking feeling.

3 **blustering** : talking in a boastful way.

4 **crestfallen** : sad because of disappointment.

5 **pusillanimous** [pjuːsɪlænɪməs] : cowardly, timid.

6 **gasped** : took a quick, deep breath of surprise.

'Sometimes, Hastings, your mental processes are amazingly quick.'

'Suppose he takes the letter with him?' 150

Poirot shook his head. 'That is very unlikely. He has evidently a hiding place in his house that he fancies to be impregnable.'

'When do we-er do the deed?'

'Tomorrow night. We will start from here about eleven o'clock.'

At the time appointed I was ready to set off. I had donned [1] a dark suit 155
and a soft dark hat. Poirot beamed [2] kindly on me.

'You have dressed the part, I see,' he observed. 'Come, let us take the underground to Wimbledon.'

'Aren't we going to take anything with us? Tools to break in with?'

'My dear Hastings, Hercule Poirot does not adopt such crude methods.' 160

It was midnight when we entered the small suburban garden of Buona Vista. The house was dark and silent. Poirot went straight to a window at the back of the house, raised the sash noiselessly, and bade me enter.

'How did you know this window would be open?' I whispered, for really it seemed uncanny. [3] 165

'Because I saw through the catch this morning.'

'What?'

'But yes, it was the most simple. I called, presented a fictitious card and one of Inspector Japp's official ones. I said I had been sent, recommended by Scotland Yard, to attend to some burglarproof fastenings that Mr. Lavington 170
wanted fixed while he was away. The housekeeper welcomed me with enthusiasm. It seems they have had two attempted burglaries here lately – evidently our little idea has occurred to other clients of Mr. Lavington's – with nothing of value taken. I examined all the windows, made my little arrangements, forbade the servants to touch the windows until tomorrow, as 175
they were electrically connected up, and withdrew gracefully.'

'Really, Poirot, you are wonderful.'

'*Mon ami*, it was of the simplest. Now, to work! The servants sleep at the top of the house, so we will run little risk of disturbing them.'

'I presume the safe is built into the wall somewhere?' 180

'Safe? Fiddlesticks! [4] There is no safe. Mr. Lavington is an intelligent man. You will see, he will have devised a hiding place much more intelligent than a safe. A safe is the first thing everyone looks for.'

1	**donned** : put on.	3	**uncanny** : odd, strange.
2	**beamed** : smiled cheerfully.	4	**Fiddlesticks!** : Nonsense!

Whereupon we began a systematic search. But after several hours'
ransacking of the house, our search had been unavailing.[1] I saw symptoms of
anger gathering on Poirot's face.

'Ah, *sapristi*, is Hercule Poirot to be beaten? Never! Let us be calm. Let us
reflect. Let us reason. Let us – *en fin*! – employ our little grey cells!'

He paused for some moments, bending his brows in concentration; then
the green light I knew so well stole into his eyes.

'I have been an imbecile! The kitchen!'

'The kitchen,' I cried. 'But that's impossible. The servants!'

'Exactly. Just what ninety-nine people out of a hundred would say! And
for that very reason the kitchen is the ideal place to choose. It is full of
various homely objects. *En avante*, to the kitchen!'

I followed him, completely sceptical, and watched while he dived into
bread bins, tapped saucepans, and put his head into the gas oven.

In the end, tired of watching him, I strolled back to the study. I was
convinced that there, and there only, would we find the *cache*. I made a
further minute search, noted that it was now a quarter past four and that
therefore it would soon be growing light, and then went back to the kitchen
regions.

To my utter amazement, Poirot was now standing right inside the coal
bin, to the utter ruin of his neat light suit. He made a grimace.

'But yes, my friend, it is against all my instincts so to ruin my appearance,
but what will you?'

'Lavington can't have buried it under the coal!'

'If you would use your eyes, you would see that it is not the coal that I
examine.'

I then saw that on a shelf behind the coal bunker[2] some logs of wood
were piled. Poirot was dexterously taking them down one by one. Suddenly
he uttered a low exclamation, 'Your knife, Hastings!'

I handed it to him. He appeared to insert it in the wood, and suddenly the
log split in two. It had been neatly sawn in half and a cavity hollowed out in
the centre. From this cavity Poirot took a little wooden box of Chinese make.

'Well done!' I cried.

'Gently, Hastings! Do not raise your voice too much. Come, let us be off
before the daylight is upon us.'

---

1   **unavailing** : unsuccessful.   2   **bunker** : container for storing coal,
fuel, etc.

Slipping the box into his pocket, he leaped lightly out of the coal bunker, brushed himself down as well as he could, and, after leaving the house by   220
the same way as we had entered, we walked rapidly in the direction of London.

'But what an extraordinary place!' I expostulated. [1] 'Anyone might have used the log.'

'In *July*, Hastings? And it was at the bottom of the pile – a very ingenious   225
hiding place. Ah, here is a taxi! Now for home, a wash, and a refreshing sleep.'

• •

6 a What is Mr Lavington like?

   b Who is Mr Japp?

   c How does Poirot manage to get into Lavington's house the first time?

   d Why does the housekeeper welcome Poirot with enthusiasm?

   e What leads Poirot to look for the box in the kitchen?

---

1   **expostulated** [ɪkspɒstjʊleitɪd] : protested.

Agatha Christie

A guessing game

7 Before reading the next part of the story try to imagine which of the characters listed below will utter the following statements:

POIROT

LADY MILLICENT

HASTINGS

JAPP

a I don't think you should have read the letter.

b Oh, how can I ever thank you! You are a wonderful, wonderful man.

c I had hoped, milady, that you would permit me to keep it – also as a souvenir.

d You nippy old devil!

e We've got your pal, too, the gentleman who called here the other day *calling himself* Lavington.

f The shoes were wrong.

8 In a group try to make predictions on how the case is going to be solved.

Read the conclusion of the story and do the activities which follow.

• •

After the excitement of the night, I slept late. When I finally strolled into our sitting room just before twelve o'clock, I was surprised to see Poirot,
230 leaning back in an armchair, the Chinese box open beside him, calmly reading the letter he had taken from it.

He smiled at me affectionately and tapped the sheet he held.

'She was right, the Lady Millicent – never would the Duke have pardoned this letter! It contains some of the most extravagant terms of affection I have
235 ever come across.'

'Really, Poirot,' I said, 'I don't think you should have read the letter. That's the sort of thing that isn't done.'[1]

'It is done by Hercule Poirot,' replied my friend imperturbably.

---

1   **That's...done** : Such things are not to be done.

168

'And another thing,' I said, 'I don't think using Japp's official card yesterday was quite playing the game.'[1]

'But I was not playing a game, Hastings. I was conducting a case.'

I shrugged – one can't argue with a point of view.

'A step on the stairs,' said Poirot. 'That will be Lady Millicent.' Our fair client came in with an anxious expression on her face which changed to one of delight on seeing the letter and box which Poirot held up.

'Oh, Monsieur Poirot, how wonderful of you! How did you do it?'

'By rather reprehensible methods, milady. But Mr. Lavington will not prosecute. This is your letter, is it not?'

She glanced through it.

'Yes. Oh, how can I ever thank you! You are a wonderful, wonderful man. Where was it hidden?'

Poirot told her.

'How very clever of you!' She took up the small box from the table. 'I shall keep this as a souvenir.'

'I had hoped, milady, that you would permit me to keep it – also as a souvenir.'

'I hope to send you a better souvenir than that – on my wedding day. You shall not find me ungrateful, Monsieur Poirot.'

'The pleasure of doing you a service will be more to me than a cheque – so you permit that I retain the box.'

'Oh, no, Monsieur Poirot, I simply must have that,' she cried laughingly.

She stretched out her hand, but Poirot's closed over it. 'I think not.' His voice had changed.

'What do you mean?' Her voice seemed to have grown sharper.

'At any rate, permit me to abstract its further contents. You observe that the original cavity has been reduced by half. In the top half, the compromising letter; in the bottom –'

He made a nimble gesture, then held out his hand. On the palm were four large glittering stones and two big milky-white pearls.

'The jewels stolen in Bond Street the other day, I rather fancy,' murmured Poirot. 'Japp will tell us.'

To my utter amazement, Japp himself stepped out of Poirot's bedroom.

'An old friend of yours, I believe,' said Poirot politely to Lady Millicent.

---

1   **playing the game** : acting correctly.

'Nabbed!' [1] said Lady Millicent with a complete change of manner. 'You nippy old devil!' [2] She looked at Poirot with almost affectionate awe.

'Well, Gertie, my dear,' said Japp, 'the game's up this time – fancy seeing you again so soon! We've got your pal, too, the gentleman who called here the other day *calling himself* Lavington. As for Lavington himself, alias Corker, alias Reed, I wonder which of the gang it was who stuck a knife into him the other day in Holland? Thought he'd got the goods with him, didn't you? And he hadn't. He double-crossed [3] you properly – hid 'em in his own house. You had two fellows looking for them, and then you tackled [4] Monsieur Poirot here, and by a piece of amazing luck he found them.'

'You do like talking, don't you?' said the late Lady Millicent. 'Easy there, now. I'll go quietly. You can't say that I'm not the perfect lady. *Ta-ta,* [5] all!'

'The shoes were wrong,' said Poirot dreamily while I was still too stupefied to speak. 'I have made my little observations of your English nation, and a lady, a born lady, is always particular about her shoes. She may have shabby [6] clothes, but she will be well shod. [7] Now, this Lady Millicent had smart, expensive clothes and cheap shoes. It was not likely that either you or I should have seen the real Lady Millicent; she has been very little in London, and this girl had a certain superficial resemblance, which would pass well enough. As I say, the shoes first awakened my suspicions, and then her story – and her veil – were a little melodramatic, eh? The Chinese box with a bogus [8] compromising letter in the top must have been known to all the gang, but the log of wood was the late Mr. Lavington's own idea. *Eh, par exemple*, Hastings, I hope you will not again wound my feelings as you did yesterday by saying that I am unknown to the criminal classes. *Ma foi*, they even employ me when they themselves fail!'

---

1   **Nabbed!** : Caught!.
2   **You nippy old devil!** : You sly old man!
3   **double-crossed** : betrayed, cheated.
4   **tackled** : (*here*) asked.
5   **Ta-ta** : Bye-bye (*informal*).
6   **shabby** : in poor condition.
7   **well shod** : wearing shoes of good quality.
8   **bogus** : false.

The Veiled Lady

An unexpected conclusion

9 a Does the outcome of the story surprise you?

b Is the conclusion plausible within the framework of the story?

Focus on how the case was solved

10 List the elements that awaken Poirot's suspicions.

11 a Why does Poirot show his desire to keep the box?

b What different names has Lavington used?

c Who is double-crossed?

d What is an English lady particular about, according to Poirot?

e How does Poirot support his idea of being well-known to the criminal classes?

Focus on language

12 What does the use of the French words/expressions add to the story?

13 Explain the meaning of the following sentences taken from the story.

	Line
When the cat is there, the little mice, they come no more to the cheese!	7-8
You know you are unique in your own line.	28
Yes, it is hardly an affair for the police.	107
It seemed to me that we had a tough nut to crack.	118-119
He has the whip hand.	121
Let us – *en fin*! – employ our little grey cells.	188
I don't think using Japp's official card yesterday was quite playing the game.	239-240

Agatha Christie

Crime-Words

14 Try to match the Crime Nouns in the box below with the following definitions.

> theft   evidence   manslaughter   psychopath
> homicide   suspect   crime   criminal
> hardened-criminal   mass-murderer   crime-wave

a situation in which there is a lot of crime

b man who is guilty of many crimes

c person suspected of a crime

d person who has killed many people

e person who has a serious disorder of character that may cause violent or criminal behaviour

f killing of one person by another

g crime of taking someone else's property from a place

h fact, sign or object which gives proof or reasons to believe or agree with something

i person who commits crimes

j offence; foolish or immoral act for which one may be punished by law

k crime of killing a person unlawfully but not intentionally

15 The following Crime Verbs have been mismatched with their definitions. Work with a partner and find the correct solution.

Blackmail   to take somebody away by force and illegally, usually to obtain money

Kidnap   to kill a human being intentionally

Hijack   to take goods secretly and illegally into or out of a country

Smuggle   to demand something (usually money) from someone by threatening to reveal information which could harm him/her

Murder   to take another person's property secretly, without permission or legal right

Steal   to seize control of a vehicle, especially an aircraft, in order to force it to go to a new destination, to take its passengers hostage or to steal its cargo

Now write down as many sentences as you can in your exercise-book, using the words you have just learnt.

The Veiled Lady

Over to you

16 What would you have done if you were Lady Millicent and Poirot did not exist?

17 Where would you have hidden the letter and the box if you were Mr Lavington?

18 In your opinion, did Hastings hurt Poirot's feelings when he said that he was unknown to the criminal world?

19 It could be said that Hastings is aware that his capabilities are limited. Support this statement by quoting some phrases from the story in which Poirot criticises Hastings.

20 Think of a different ending for the story and write it in your exercise-book.

AFTER READING

Retelling the Story

21 Write down something next to the headings below, then stand up and tell your classmates what you have written.

The .... starts with ... .
....
....
....
....

It is set in ... .
....
....
....
....

First ... .
....
....
....
....

Then ... .
....
....
....
....

Agatha Christie

After that ... .
....
....
....
....

In the end ... .
....
....
....
....

Word-File

22 Revise all the words you have met throughout the story you have just read: highlight the words which you think will be useful for communication and insert them in the following table.

Useful Words	Meaning

CROSS-CURRICULAR DATA

The Detective Story

Also known as a 'whodunit', i.e. 'who has done it?', the detective story is based on a famous detective's investigations of a crime, with the criminal being discovered at the end of the story. Where the mystery to be solved concerns a crime, the work may also be called crime fiction.

The 'investigations' are at the centre of this type of story with the detective as the main character who is well known for his detective skills: he/she judges what is right or wrong and is generally helped by a less capable friend in his/her investigations; the 'friend' is normally unable to see things as quickly and clearly as the detective. In this type of story the reader is usually given enough information to solve the puzzle or to discover who the murderer is.

The 'golden age' of this genre was the period from the 1920s to the 1940s, when the leading writers were women – Agatha Christie, Margery Allingham and Dorothy L. Sayers. Types of detective fiction include 'the police procedural' where the mystery is solved by detailed police work, as in the work of Swedish writers Maj Sjowall and Per Wahloo; 'the inverted novel' where the identity of the criminal is known from the beginning, and only the method or the motive remains to be discovered, as in *Malice Aforethought* by Francis Iles; and 'the hard-boiled school' of private investigators begun by Raymond Chandler and Dashiell Hammett, which became known for its social realism and explicit violence.

Outstanding Works:

The Murders in the Rue Morgue (1841) by Edgar Allan Poe: the detective Dupin was the first literary detective who solved crimes by deduction.

A Study in Scarlet (1887) by Arthur Conan Doyle: the detective Sherlock Holmes and his assistant Dr Watson first appeared in this story.

The Murder of Roger Ackroyd (1926) by Agatha Christie: a story in which the narrator is the murderer.

Note down:

1   the subject matter of the detective story.

2   the reasons why the detective stands out from the other characters.

3   what is unusual in *The Murder of Roger Ackroyd* (1926).

OVERVIEW

A Reference-Table

1 Copy this table onto a double page of your exercise book, then complete it referring to the whole book.

	author	text-type	setting	characters	themes	narrator	language
Dracula							
Earthbound							
Carlotta							
'Tain't So							
The Man Who Loved Flowers							
Mr Loveday's Little Outing							
The Tell-Tale Heart							
The Robot Who Wanted to Know							
The Hobbyist							
The Veiled Lady							

Compare/contrast what you have written with a partner.

Framing Characters

2 Complete the following chart on the characters you have read about in the book.

Title	Characters presented in a sympathetic way	Characters presented in a critical way
Dracula		
Earthbound		
Carlotta		
'Tain't So		
The Man Who Loved Flowers		
Mr Loveday's Little Outing		
The Tell-Tale Heart		
The Robot Who Wanted to Know		
The Hobbyist		
The Veiled Lady		

3 If you look back at the Contents page, you will realise that the characters of this book have been divided into three groups. Which of the three groups of characters appeals to you the most? Why?

Your Favourite Characters

4 Choose three characters that you particularly liked in the book and insert as much information as you can in the following table.

	Physical Appearance	Personality	Behaviour	Reasons why I like him/her
Character 1				
Character 2				
Character 3				

Flat and Round Characters

The characters of a fictional text may be flat or round.

A **FLAT** character or 'type' is built around a single idea and s/he is normally 'static', which means that there is little or no development or change in his/her personality or behaviour, as the story progresses.

A **ROUND** character is more harmonious and complete: s/he undergoes physical/ psychological changes throughout the story.

Overview

5 Decide whether the main chaacters of the stories you have read are flat or round and write their names in the correct column of the Chart below.

Flat	Round

6 Which category predominates? To what effect?

Writing

7 Select one character and write about the way in which his/her relationship with the other character/s of the same story shows you what kind of person s/he is.

8 Imagine a meeting between two characters from different stories. Invent a story, write it down, then stand up and tell your classmates what you have written. Try to keep the characters consistent with their own personalities, behaviour, etc.

Over to You

9 Answer the following questions.

a At the beginning of the book there is a Panoramic View on the origins, development and varieties of the short story and some stories are followed by Cross-Curricular Data.

Have you found all the sections useful/important/essential/necessary/irrelevant/ boring, etc.? Do you think they have made you a more competent reader? Why/why not?

b Do you think that the Information on the authors is useful for understanding the texts, or not?

c To what extent have the Word-Files at the end of each story helped to make you a more autonomous reader?

d How have the Recordings improved your general knowledge/comprehension/ appreciation of the texts?

Discuss your answers with your teacher and classmates.

BIBLIOGRAPHY

AA. VV., *Dictionary of English Language and Culture*, Longman, 1992

AA. VV., *Webster's Concise Interactive Encyclopedia*, Attica Cybernetics, 1994

AA. VV., *Cinemania*, Microsoft Corporation, 1996

ALDERSON J. C. and URQUART A. H., *Reading in a Foreign Language*, Longman, 1992

BASSNET S. and GRUNDY P., *Language through Literature*, Longman, 1993

BURTON S. H., *Mastering Practical Writing*, MacMillan, 1987

COLLIE J. and SLATER S., *Listening*, Cambridge University Press, 1993

COOK G., *Discourse and Literature*, Oxford University Press, 1994

DE LUCA, GRILLO, PACE, RANZOLI, *Literature and Beyond 1*, Loescher, 1997

DUFF A. and MALEY A., *Literature*, Oxford University Press, 1990

HOPKINS A., *Perspectives*, Longman, 1994

HORNBY A. S., *Oxford Advanced Learner's Dictionary*, Oxford University Press, 1989

LEECH G. N. and SHORT M. H., *Style in Fiction*, Arco Press, 1988

MC RAE J., *Words on Words*, Loffredo-Napoli, 1990

MINGAZZINI, SALMOIRAGHI, SADLEIR, *A Mirror of the Times: American Section*, Morano, 1989

MORGAN J. and RINVOLUCRI M., *Vocabulary*, Oxford University Press, 1986

SPIAZZI M. and TAVELLA M., *Only Connect 3*, Zanichelli, 1997

THORNLEY G. C. and ROBERTS G., *An Outline of English Literature*, Longman, 1993

WELLMAN G., *Wordbuilder*, Heinemann, 1989